SCHOLASTIC

The Big Book of Classroom Poems

BY KATHLEEN M. HOLLENBECK

NEW YORK • TORONTO • LONDON • AUCKLAND • SYDNEY
MEXICO CITY • NEW DELHI • HONG KONG • BUENOS AIRES

Teaching Resources

To Sarah Morry,
Dr. Robert Legare,
Reverend Michael Menna,
Dr. Dana Chofay,
and Dr. Maureen Chung
with gratitude for your wisdom,
commitment, and compassion.

To a place of darkness
few may understand,
comes a firm assurance
and a gentle hand.
Guided by such efforts,
ground so kindly tilled
reaps the joyous harvest
of a dream fulfilled.

Thank you.

Front cover and interior design by Kathy Massaro
Cover art by Katherine Lucas
Interior illustrations by Dawn Apperly, Mike Gordon, James Graham Hale, Mark Hicks, and Bari Weissman

ISBN 0-439-43826-8

Published by Scholastic Inc.

Printed in the U.S.A.

3 4 5 6 7 8 9 10 40 11 10 09 08 07 06 05

contents

Science • 83

Introduction

When I was eight years old, I wrote a poem for a third-grade language assignment. While not an amazing piece of literature, that poem became important to me. Its creation marked the exact moment my passion for words came alive and proved the spark that ignited a lifelong devotion to writing.

Today in your classroom, you have the opportunity to spark in your students feelings of enthusiasm, excitement, comfort, and compassion. You can foster a love of words, guide students in recognizing meter and rhyme, strengthen their reading skills, and broaden their awareness of the world around them . . . all through the use of poetry.

Inside this book, you'll find more than 240 fun, easy-to-read poems, each linked with a learning element from the primary curriculum and designed to appeal to students in kindergarten through grade 3. Often written from a child's point of view, the poems entertain and inspire, probe and present, ask and apply. As you share the poems with students, you'll tickle your tongues and weave your way through a maze of verse that touches on hundreds of subjects familiar and important to young minds. You'll flit with a housefly, absorb the essence of the four seasons, and meet word families up close.

Poems dealing with key topics in language arts, math, science, social studies, character development, and the arts fill these pages. Open this book and step in to discover that poetry in line with the needs and interests of its audience can expand the experience of language, and any topic under the sun—or even around it!

Why Use Poetry?

- **Poetry Tells It Like It Is.** Poems cover every topic imaginable, in depth or on the surface. Meant to explore and explain, poems can make difficult subjects easy to understand and the obvious even more so.

- **Poems Come in All Shapes and Sizes—Literally!** From haiku to ballad, they vary in length and depth. They can be three lines or thirty-three, providing abundant detail or just a bit.

- **Poetry Builds Reading Fluency.** Poetry offers endless opportunities to practice key aspects of fluency such as phrasing, intonation, punctuation, and vocabulary. Many poems carry a lyrical, sometimes predictable rhythm that practically rolls off the tongue, making them fun to read aloud, pleasant to hear, and easy to follow along.

- **There's a Poem for Everyone.** While not every poem will appeal to every reader, somewhere, somehow, every reader who seeks will most certainly find at least one that grabs his attention or tickles her funny bone.

- **Poetry Waltzes With Words.** Within the walls of a poem exist opportunities to examine the use of phonics, parts of speech, alliteration, metaphor, patterning, meter, placement, rhyme, and a host of other lingual elements.
- **Poetry Strengthens Communication Skills.** As students share poetry, they can't help but bolster skills in reading, listening, and speaking.

Teachers reach for poetry,
and lessons come alive,
illuminating history
and how to count to five,
describing common feelings
or sharing silly tales,
identifying elephants,
exploring ants and whales.
No matter what the topic,
how stately or absurd,
when teachers reach for poetry,
they know they will be heard.

Ways to Use Poems in the Classroom

Poetry, by its very nature, begs to be shared, and there are dozens of ways to do that in the classroom. Look over the suggestions below and choose the ones that will appeal most to you and your students.

- **Read Aloud Often.** Read poems aloud, and have students read to you. You can gauge their comprehension by observing how they recite. *Do they use appropriate expression? Is their timing on track? Do they pick up on the meter and potential rhyme scheme of the poem?*
- **Enjoy Rather Than Analyze.** In the primary grades, cultivating a love of literature and poetry holds more importance than focusing on mechanics. As much as possible, help students notice and appreciate poetry for the way it sounds, the images it depicts, and the emotion it conveys.
- **Where's the Rhyme?** Explore the use of different rhyme schemes, as in "How Many?" (page 69), "Hail" (page 95), "My Apple Tree" (page 123), and "Mittens, Hat, or Boots" (page 133). Discuss the idea that rhyming poems do not always employ the same rhyme scheme; the rhyme can come at the end of a line, in the middle of a sentence, or any place where the poet feels it best serves the sound and the course of the poem.

Plan a Pocket Chart. As a teacher of young children, you know well that poetry and pocket charts go hand in hand. Many of the poems in this book are perfect for pocket charts. Write each line of a selected poem on a tagboard strip, and place the lines in order in your pocket chart. Then:

- **Match Missing Portions of the Poem.** Cover the animal baby names in the poem "Animal Babies" (page 102). Write the name of each animal baby on its own strip of tagboard, and have students match the name of each baby to its mother.

- **Reach for Riddles.** On small strips of tagboard, write or draw the answers to riddles such as those in "Peek Into the Pond" (page 110). Invite students to place each animal or insect with the riddle that describes it.

- **Make a Rebus.** Turn any poem into a rebus by replacing—or asking students to replace—specific words of the poem with pictures. The poem "Outside Antonyms" (page 54) offers nearly a dozen rebus opportunities.

Up With Acrostics! Invite students to model a poem or two after the language poems "Person, Place, or Thing?" and "Verbs" (page 52), or "Ants" (page 116), which are acrostics. Students can create acrostics (poems in which the first letter of each line combine to spell a word vertically) using virtually any noun in the English language as the subject, including their own names.

Try Tongue Twisters. Many of the poems in the alphabet section of this book can be used as tongue twisters. Invite students to select words from the poems—or any words they like—to make their own tongue twisters for classmates to recite. Looking for one to get you started? Try "The Letter F" (page 26).

Sound It Out! Inspire students to write poems describing the sounds they hear in real life. The *hissssss* of a whistling teapot and the *whhhooo* of a cold winter wind bring winter to mind.

Make a Mobile. Use a poem as the model for a mobile your students can make and hang in the classroom. Choose a poem that describes a variety of items, such as "Planet Panic" (page 101), which names the nine planets and tells fictitious tales about them. Have students cut and color tagboard circles to represent the planets and the sun. Using string, suspend these at different lengths from a clothes hanger. (Hang the planets in order according to their distance from the sun.) On each planet, have students glue a conversation bubble that tells what the planet might have said to express the way it felt in the poem.

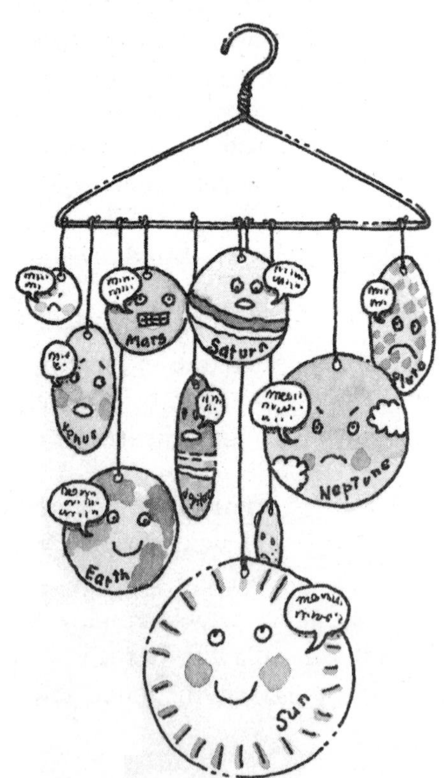

Try Haiku and Tanka. Haiku offers children a way to write without trying to rhyme or arrange words on the page. In haiku, writers determine word choice and placement according to the number of syllables per line. Haiku usually involves reference to nature and contains the syllable pattern 5-7-5 (5 in the first line, 7 in the second line, 5 in the last). Explore this poetry form with "The Sun" and "The Moon" (page 99) and "Winter in the Park" and "Smooth" (page 131). Tanka, similar to haiku but longer in length, often follows a similar syllable pattern: 5-7-5-7-7. Examples of tanka include "Raindrops" (page 93), "Recycle" (page 98), and "Winter Storm" (page 134).

Create a Poetry Wreath. Cut 4-inch shapes of any kind (stars, circles, pumpkins, and so on) from sturdy construction paper. Cut the center circle from a 9-inch paper plate, and use the outside as the base of a poetry wreath. Have students copy the lines or verses of a poem onto different shapes. Then help them glue or staple the shapes onto the wreath, placing them in order (clockwise) to duplicate the original poem.

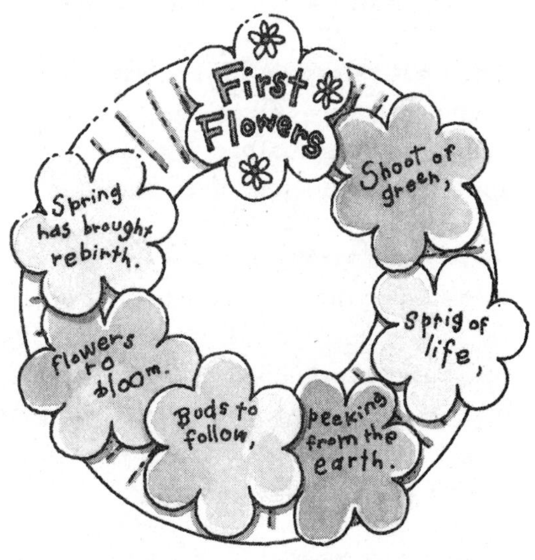

Put Poems on Display. Write the verses of a poem on any shape that fits with your classroom motif, and post it on a wall at students' eye level. For example, you might write verses on a string of railroad cars, a group of ducklings following their mother, or a bunch of balloons in the sky.

Use Poems for Movement. "At the Zoo" (page 105) calls for creative movement, with instructions alongside the poem. Ask students to act out other poems as well, dramatizing poems such as "Seating Trouble" (page 20) and "Checking My Work" (page 23).

Bring Imagery to Life. The poem "Scarecrow" (page 129) describes a simple, homemade scarecrow in a field. Provide craft sticks, fabric swatches, glue, and yarn, and direct students to make the scarecrow they envisioned as they listened to the poem. You might also want to provide chalk for them to recreate the swirls and designs described in "Frost" (page 132) or clay to recreate some of the animals named in the poems on page 103.

Paint Poetry Placemats. Reproduce a poem and ask students to illustrate it, using colorful markers or crayons. Laminate each student's page to make a placemat for snack time.

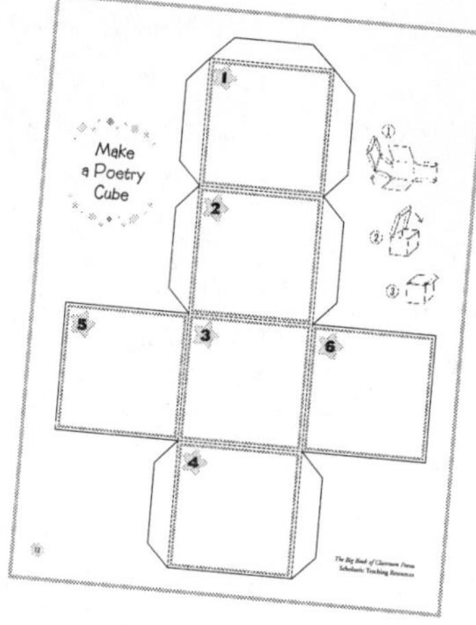

Make a Poetry Cube. Photocopy the reproducible "Make a Poetry Cube" (page 12) and distribute it to students. Have them write each line (or verse, depending on the length of the selection) on one square of the cube, beginning at square number 1. Then fold up the cube as directed, tape in place, and turn it to recite the poem.

Post a Poem-of-the-Day. Choose a poem a day to write on the chalkboard near the day's assignments. Incorporate the poem into your morning routine, just as you may already do with the hot lunch count and today's weather.

Work With Word Families. Write the word family poems (pages 37–50) on chart paper. Invite students to circle the words from each family, replace them with other words from the family wherever possible, and make word family mini-books, bookmarks, and scrapbooks.

Head Out on a Word Hunt! Build word recognition and emphasize parts of speech by setting student detectives on a hunt for specific words in the poems. In "Person, Place, or Thing," "Verbs," and "Adjectives" (page 52), have students use highlighters to mark the nouns, verbs, or adjectives they find. In other poems, send them searching for words to add to a thematic word wall (words that describe heroes, have to do with planting, name vehicles, and so on).

Change the Words. Dozens of the poems offer chances to replace nouns, verbs, and adjectives with synonyms or simply other words of the same part of speech. For example, in the poem "Verbs" (page 52), the words *eat, rescue,* and *be* can be easily replaced by words such as *share, cuddle,* and *hug.* In "Just Alike" (page 54), challenge students to replace one of the synonyms in each line with a word that means the same thing.

Home in on Homonyms and Antonyms. "Seaside Homonyms" (page 53) contains four homonym pairs (*pale/pail, to/two, our/hour,* and *sea/see*), but has additional words that have a homonym partner not mentioned. (Examples include *we/wee, there/their, not/knot, for/four, and in/inn.*) Challenge students to find both the homonym pairs and the would-be homonyms. In "Outside Antonyms" (page 54), have them replace the object of each antonym with a different object that fits with the adjective. For example, instead of *The sun is hot. The snow is cold,* students might write *The stove is hot. The fridge is cold.*

Move Into Math. Learning-rich opportunities abound using the math poems in this book. Some suggestions follow:

- Extend the counting activity in math poems such as "New Crayons" (page 62) and "Window Math" (page 63) by having students count up the crayons and windows in your classroom.

- Substitute the math sums and differences in "Number Families" (page 65) to review newly learned math facts. (The poem has been set up to allow for substitution.)
- Look for additional real-life shapes to go with "Schoolroom Shapes" (page 65), real-life student bodies to replicate the pattern in "Who's Next?" (page 67), and students' own footwear to duplicate that described in "Sneakers in Line" (page 68). At the end of "Sneakers in Line," readers are challenged to figure out how many pairs of each kind of sneaker the class had if they had 20 pairs in all. To complete the pattern, the class would need to put down two more pairs of sneakers that closed with Velcro, six more pairs with laces, and three more pairs of slip-ons.
- To accompany "Overflow" (page 72), fill two different-sized glasses with the same amount of water and note how the same volume of water can appear different. Also, add the same amount of water to two identical glasses and then add several rocks or ice cubes to one. What happens?
- For a genuine reenactment of "Cupcake Math" (page 75), bake cupcakes and let the class brainstorm ways to divide them so that each child will get an equal serving that includes some portion of frosting. (Cut the cupcakes in half!)

Shape a Subject. Examine the shape poems "Blowing a Bubble" (page 21), and "Water and Ice" (page 95). Have students write their own shape poems, emphasizing the idea that they can be rhyming or non-rhyming.

Tell It on a Time Line. Help your students make a time line to record the events of a day at the beach, as described in the poem "Beach Day" (page 140).

Riddle Answer Keys

"-*an* Riddles" (page 39): pan, fan, man

"-*ash* Riddles" (page 40): sash, ash, mash, cash

"-*aw* Riddles" (page 42): jaw, straw, paw, law

"-*est* Riddles" (page 44): rest, best, test, vest

"-*ill* Riddles" (page 46): hill, ill, will, still

"-*ore* Riddles" (page 49): chore, store, bore, snore

"Bike Safety Rule Riddles" (page 87): helmet, street, light, one

"What Animal Am I?" (page 109): hen, pig, rooster, horse, cow, sheep

"Peek Into the Pond" (page 110): dragonfly, frog, bug, fish, snail

"Where Will I Go?" (page 155) restaurant; shoe store; library or bookstore; candy store; supermarket; laundromat; train station, bus station or airport; pet store

"Who Am I?" (page 156) baker, pilot, bus driver or taxi driver, dentist, mail carrier, teacher, veterinarian, hairdresser or barber

"What Symbol Am I?" (page 158): American flag, bald eagle, Statue of Liberty, Uncle Sam

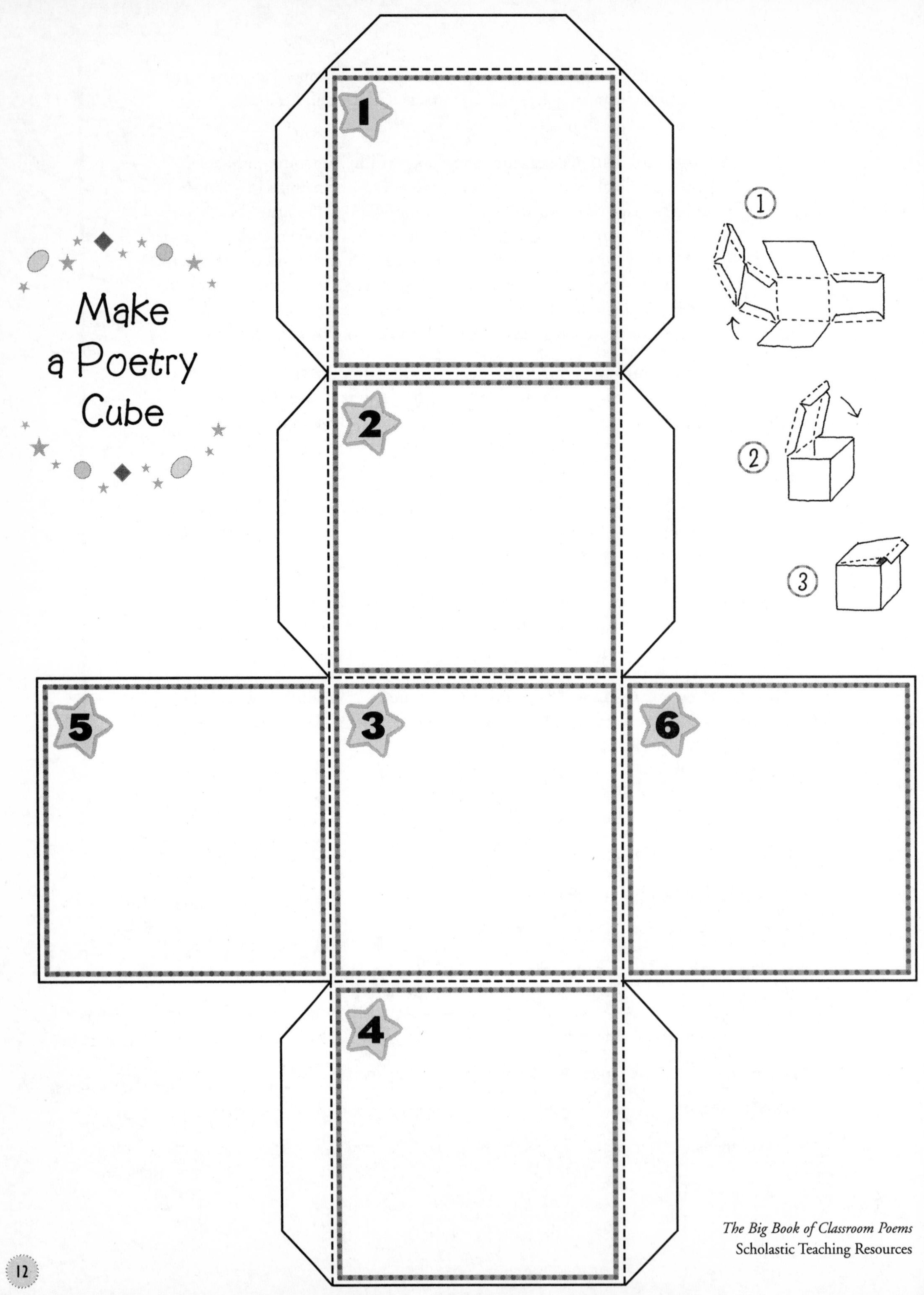
Make a Poetry Cube
1
2
3
4
5
6
1
2
3

School Supplies

I filled my supply box with markers and tape,
pencils, erasers, and glue,
scissors, a ruler, erasable pens.
Now I can't close it. Can you?

Deep in My Desk

Deep in my desk,
under papers and pencils
and tissues and folders and glue,
wedged between homework
and crumpled art projects
and maybe an old snack or two,
somewhere among all the
markers and crayons
and library books overdue,
there is a math book I need right away.
Yes! There's the edge of it! Phew!

Classroom Helper

I want to help.
What can I do?
Erase the board
and wash it, too?
Clap erasers?
Sweep the floor?
Pass out straws?
Hold the door?
Put the recess
balls away?
Lead the class at
Pledge today?
I see my name.
What job is mine?
Hurrah!
I get to lead the line!

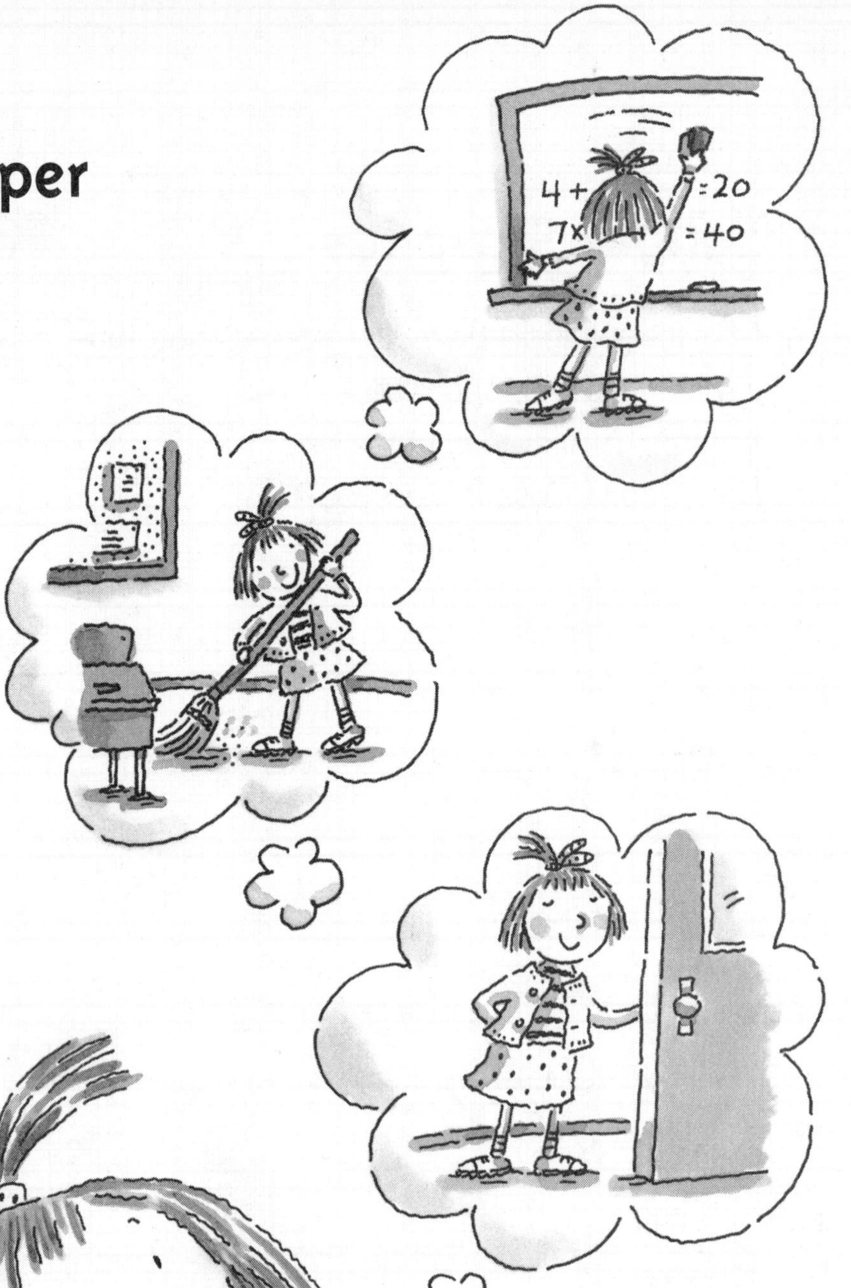

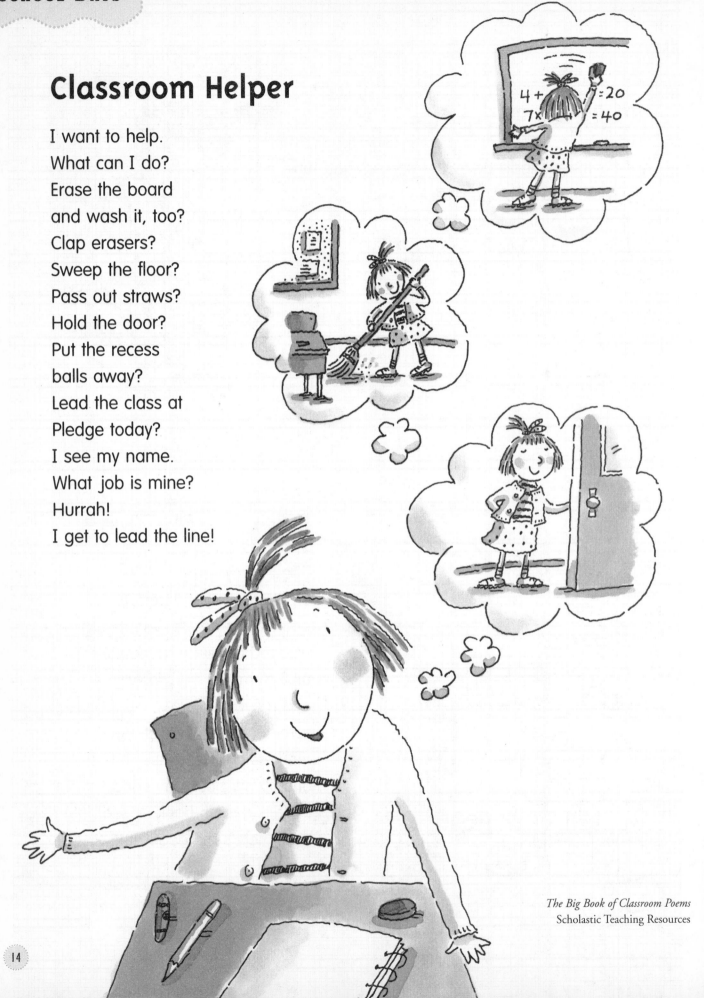

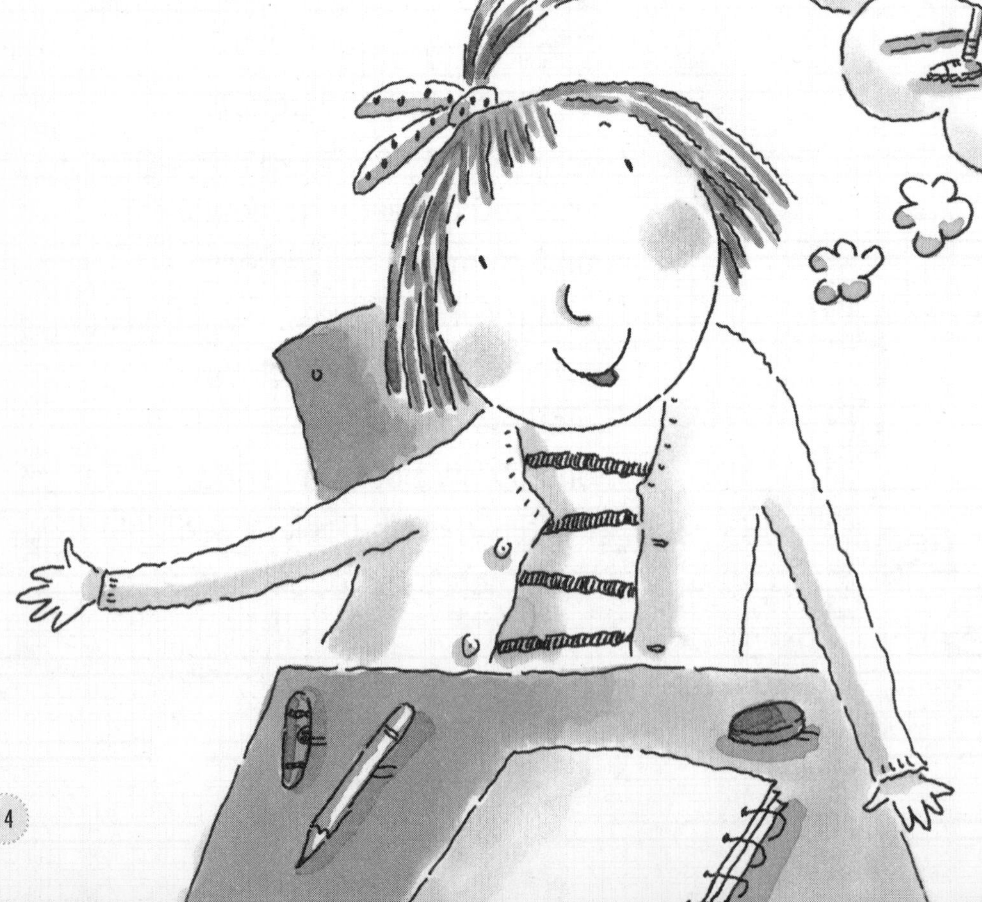

The Substitute Teacher

When I got to school today,
my teacher wasn't there.
Someone else was at her desk
and sitting in her chair.
She didn't have my teacher's smile
        or hands
                or hair
                        or voice.
She didn't ask if she could stay.
I didn't have a choice.
Her smile was warm and friendly.
She told us all her name.
She taught us math and phonics.
We played a spelling game.
She read a funny chapter book
and had us read some, too.
She did just about everything
our own teacher would do.
I learned a lot at school today.
I had a lot of fun.
If my teacher's out again,
I hope we get this one!

Fire Drill

Quietly we sat,
concentrating well,
adding and subtracting.
THEN WE HEARD A BELL!
It was like no other,
loud and long and shrill.
"Line up!" said our teacher.
"IT'S A FIRE DRILL!
Leave your books and pencils.
Stand up right away.
Don't take coats or backpacks.
EVERYTHING MUST STAY."
In a line, we hurried,
walking as a class,
straight across the pavement
OVER TO THE GRASS.
Every class stood out there.
All was strangely still.
There we were, a school on hold
FOR A FIRE DRILL.

Open House

Welcome to our classroom!
Come in! Sit down and stay.
Learn what it is we're learning.
See how we spend our day.

On the Move

My pencil's looking dull again.
My throat feels awfully dry.
I have to use the bathroom.
Is there something in my eye?

Imagine all the work I'd do
if I stayed in my seat.
Yet somehow, I keep finding ways
to get up on my feet.

Hoping for a Snow Day

Snowflakes falling
through the night,
comforter of icy white,
thick enough for snowsuit play,
but not for schools to close today.
Standing at the bus stop—
WAIT.
Maybe school's an hour late?
Then a sound we sadly know...
school bus tires on the snow.

Indoor Recess

It's raining and we can't go out for recess.
Inside games will have to do today.
I-Spy? Bingo? Seven-Up?
Checkers? Puzzles? Hide-the-Pup?
What games do you really like to play?

The Hall

I need to use the bathroom
but it isn't lunch or snack.
I take the bathroom hall pass
and I say I'll hurry back.
I step into the hallway,
close the door, and look around.
No one else is out here.
There is not a single sound.
It's really kind of special
being out here on my own.
The hall looks so much longer
when you're in it all alone.
It's calm and still and peaceful,
and I feel a little free
just being in the hallway
without someone watching me.

Seating Trouble

I really liked the place I sat
near Juan and Bill and Nate.
We always talked and laughed a lot,
and it was really great.
My teacher said we talked too much
and warned us to be still.
We didn't listen very well,
so one day, she moved Bill.
We tried our best to do our work
and to participate.
Then came the paper airplane fleet.
That morning, she moved Nate.
Juan and I were good as gold
until one fateful day.
Who would have thought a book could fly?
She dragged my desk away.
Here I sit, alone up front,
and now from 8 to 2,
I only pay attention
for there's nothing else to do.

My Lunch Box

My lunch box sits
upon the shelf.
I look with longing eyes.
It sits there like
a treasure box
that holds a great surprise.
The lunch bell rings.
I race across
and grab my box and then
I open it...
excitement fades...
it's tuna fish again.

Blowing a Bubble

Sticky, sweet, and soft. Flat and thin and ready. Slowly, gently fills with air. Bigger...bigger...POP!

What Makes a Winner?

Ten math problems on the test.
I try to do them fast.
It looks like Jen's ahead of me.
I don't want to be last.
I do the first five quickly,
and then I start to guess.
I'm not sure what I'm doing now.
My paper is a mess.
I rush through numbers nine and ten
and hand my paper in.
Forgot my name. I lose five points,
but I am first. I win!
Or did I . . . ?
Today, I find I got three wrong,
skipped one, and failed the test.
Why did I try to be the first?
I wish I'd done my best.

Checking My Work

Before I hand my paper in,
I check it out to see
if I've followed all the rules
my teacher's asked of me.
Did I sign my name on top?
Is my handwriting neat?
Did I fill in all the answers?
Are my sentences complete?
Did I check my answers to
be sure I didn't guess?
I can hand my paper in
if all of these are "Yes."

The Letter 

A is for acorn
and sweet apple pie,
attic and angel and
arrows that fly.

A sounds can be long
as in ate, ape, and aim,
or short as in Annie,
which is someone's name.

The Letter 

Baseball, banjo, bed, and better,
these words share the same first letter.
Beetle, bathtub...do you see?
Each word starts with letter B.

Ball, banana, box, and back,
colors such as brown and black,
basket, bumblebee, and birds,
B begins each of these words.

The Letter C

Cabin, cactus, comb, and cake
show one sound that C can make.
Camel, cup, and candy bar
share the same first sound as car.

Citrus, circus, and city
use the softer side of C.
In fact, when C is paired with I,
the soft sound is the one to try.

The Letter D

D is for dancer and doughnut and dew,
daisy and dandelion, daffodil, too.
Doorbell and duckling and donkey and day;
each one begins in the very same way.

D can put dozens of words in your head,
whether in daylight or darkness you tread.
Daddy and daughter and dove you will see
when out finding words that begin with a D.

The Letter E

Elephant, envelope, egg, and elbow
start in the same way as elf and echo.
Eagle, eraser, and eardrum, you see,
also begin with the same letter: E.

Engine and earthquakes that rattle the ground
are two more examples that E makes a sound.
Emerald and enemy, eel and elm tree.
What other E words can you share with me?

The Letter F

A fish has fins. A fox has fur.
A finch has downy feathers.
Fireflies light up the sky
when they all flash together.

A frog is fairly fond of flies.
A fawn, afraid, will flee.
What other words that start with F
do you think there might be?

The Letter G

G makes a hard sound in goldfish and geese,
grandmother, garden, and graph.
G makes a soft sound in giant and gel,
gingerbread, gee, and giraffe.

Hard is the G that starts guppies and game,
giggle, gorilla, and gum.
Words with soft G aren't as easy to find.
Gem, germ, and gentle are some.

The Letter H

If H had a house,
who might live there?
A hippo? A hamster?
A hen or a hare?

A hog or hyena?
A hornet? A horse?
What would they eat?
Hamburgers, of course!

The Letter I

For inch and insect,
ink and indeed,
short I is the sound
you need.

Ice and idea
and iron. My!
These are words
that use long I.

The Letter J

Have you ever tried juggling J words?
Like jiggle and jingle and jet?
Just try it! Recite them together.
It's a job that your tongue won't forget.

Try jellyfish, jungle, and justice.
Then jacket and janitor, too.
Now join them together and say them all fast.
Such jumble! How well did you do?

The Letter 

Kitten, key, and kingdom,
kite that flies away,
kiss and kind and kettle.
These words start with K.

Kindergarten, kitchen,
kelp, and kangaroo,
kick and keep and keyboard.
These are K words, too.

The Letter 

L is a letter that we like to hear.
Listen! These words start with L:
log, leaf, and laughter,
lazy and lie,
lightning, and lettuce, as well.

Ladder and lady and lamp and lagoon,
lizard and lobster and lose.
You need not look far to find
words you can list
when L is the letter you choose.

The Letter M

Mat and marble, macaroni,
mail and meatball,
moss and mice.
These are words that start with M,
and each of them is rather nice.

Movie, monkey, melon, mitten,
mound and meadow,
minnow, too.
Even cows can make the M sound,
as they loudly cry out "M-m-m-OO!!"

The Letter N

Newspaper, noodle, and needle and nest
nibble and narrow and name,
nighttime and napkin and noodle and nut...
how are these words all the same?

Naptime and nephew and notebook and next,
have much in common somehow.
Each of them starts with the same letter: N.
Why don't you try them right now?

The Letter O

Short O starts ostrich and olive and ox,
octopus, otter, and on.
You hear a short O in often and odd,
officer, and octagon.

We use long O for oasis and old,
ocean and oat and obey.
Over and open share long O, as well.
That's all we'll say now. Okay?

The Letter P

If you pack a picnic lunch,
give letter P a try.
Put in peanuts, pasta, and
a piece of pumpkin pie.

Add a pile of pancakes and
perhaps some pears and peas.
If you plan to spend the night,
then pack pajamas, please!

The Letter Q

Quick and quiet, quail and queen,
quarter, quilt, and quiz.
These begin with letter Q.
That's the way it is.

These, along with quack and quit,
show that letter Q
almost never stands alone.
It belongs with U.

The Letter R

Race and rabbit and raccoon,
rag and rain and rise.
Each begins with letter R,
as does realize.

Rope and roses, roam and roar,
Robe and road and row.
These are really R words, too,
just like radio.

The Letter S

If I sold S words in a store,
some of them might be
sat and saddle, sack and saw,
sailor, salt, and sea.

Season, seesaw, scold, and save,
sandwich, sail, and shell.
In a shop made just for S,
these are words I'd sell.

The Letter T

Tiptoe to my table
and try a cup of tea.
Taste a toasted muffin.
Take time to talk with me.

Tell me when you're tired,
at ten or twelve or three.
We'll set up a tiny tent
and rest beneath a tree.

The Letter U

What kinds of words start with U?
Uncle and under and use,
understand, upstairs, unusual.
Any of these you may choose.

U starts unhappy and underwear,
ugly, unless, and untie.
You won't find U very useful
until you give it a try.

The Letter 

I went on vacation last summer
to a village I visit a lot.
The village lies deep in a valley
near a very big vegetable plot.

First I was only a visitor,
but then I decided to stay.
Now I am here all but three months a year,
from Veterans to Valentine's Day.

The Letter 

What will we do
when the wind isn't warm
and the weather is cloudy and wet?
We'll watch out the window
while ocean waves grow.
We'll wonder how big they will get.

When spring arrives,
the winter has ended.
We know warmer weather's at hand.
We'll wander together
with boots on our feet
and wade where the waves meet the land.

The Letter 

I hear the X sound
In x-ray and ox,
exit, examine, and
boxes and fox.

The word xylophone
is surprising to me,
for in that word, X
makes the same sound as Z!

The Letter Y

Yesterday I cooked a yellow egg yolk
    and a yam.
They looked so good
    I could not wait to eat.
Yet, I never ate them
    for a dog came in my yard.
He ate my meal and ran off down the street.

The Letter Z

What words start with letter Z?
More than just a few.
Zebra, zigzag, zip, and zoom,
zero, zone, and zoo.

Zipper, zany, zap, and zeal,
zodiac, and zinc,
plus a few hard words to say.
That is all, I think.

Jack

A little boy named Jack
felt hungry for a snack
while riding on a train
into town and back.
Click-clack! Click-clack! Click-clack!
He opened up a sack
and feasted as the train
sped along the track.

A Snail

I found a small snail
beneath a sand pail.
I saw the shell only
and no head or tail.
I waited all day
but to no avail.
For each time I looked,
he hid without fail.

A Train

An old, rusty train
was hooked to a chain
and pulled up a hillside in Spain.
A hole in the roof
let in lots of rain.
A hole in the floor was a drain.

When I Wake

Tomorrow when I wake
I plan to bake a cake
and take it on a picnic
by the lake.
They say it's going to snow.
What difference will that make?
I'm going even if I
see a flake.

-an Riddles

Try these little riddles.
Solve them if you can.

First, where might you cook an egg?
In a frying _____________.

When you're hot and sweating,
you turn on a _____________.

When a little boy grows up,
he is called a _____________.

Little Hank

Little Hank took money
from his piggy bank
and bought himself a goldfish.
He put it in a tank.
Instead of eating fish food,
the goldfish only drank,
and he became so heavy,
he sank
and sank
and sank.

Clap! Flap! Tap!

Come on, everybody!
Put your hands together. Clap!
Now bend your elbows twice
and flap, flap, flap!
Focus on your right foot.
Make it tap, tap, tap!
Wow! I'm really tired now.
I think I'll take a nap.

-ash Riddles

What you tie around your waist
is called a belt or ______________.

After wood has burned,
it leaves behind a pile of ______________.

When you whip potatoes
you might also say you ______________.

When you pay with dollar bills,
you say you pay in ______________.

A Cat and a Rat

Chat with me a while
and I'll tell you of a cat
who fell asleep
while lying on a mat.
As he slept, a rat
crept up to him and sat
and chewed the mat to bits.
Imagine that!

A Date for Dinner

Once, when night was falling
and the hour growing late,
my mom gave me a date to eat.
She put it on my plate.
I didn't know just what it was.
I asked my sister Kate.
She'd had a date for dinner, too,
and that was all she ate.

-aw Riddles

The bones of your mouth
form your ____________.

You drink lemonade
through a ____________.

A puppy dog's foot
is a ____________.

A rule to obey
is a ____________.

A Cold Gray Day

Yesterday was cold and gray.
We all stayed inside to play.
We made puppets out of clay
and put on a show.
If it's cold again today,
and if the clouds decide to stay,
we'll go outside anyway.
Maybe it will snow!

In the Heat

To crops out wilting
in the heat,
a summer rain
is quite a treat.
As raindrops drum
a steady beat,
the plants stand tall,
from corn to wheat.

The Sheep's Jeep

Fifteen white sheep
climbed into a jeep
and rode to the top
of a hill that was steep.
All the way up,
not one made a peep.
But all the way down,
they pressed the horn:
BEEP!

Nell and the Shell

A little blue crab named Nell
crawled into a giant sea shell.
The shell, dark and winding,
was really worth finding.
Inside it, Nell slept very well!

-est Riddles

Try to go to bed on time.
Give your body ______________.

Wash your face and brush your hair.
Try to look your ______________.

Study what you need to know
when you have a ______________.

When the air is rather cool,
wear a coat or ______________.

Mice Are Nice

Of all the animals I know,
the most polite are mice.
They ask how you are feeling.
They're almost always nice.
If you share a pie with them,
you get the biggest slice.
They listen well and never tell.
They give out wise advice.

The Ocean Wide

The ocean stretches
far and wide.
Above the waves,
the sea gulls glide.
They dive into
the rolling tide
and catch the fish
that cannot hide.

The Moon Tonight

The moon is bright tonight
tonight
and shines a silvery light
a light
that never fades from sight
from sight
till night has taken
flight.

-ill Riddles

A grassy slope
is called a ______________.

If you are sick,
then you are ______________.

The opposite of won't
is ______________.

When you don't move,
you're staying ______________.

Nine Swine

Nine swine hung onto a vine
and soared over maple
and elm tree
and pine.

When they were done,
they might have looked fine,
but not one was able
to walk a straight line.

A Swing in the Spring

On a bright sunny day in the spring,
a bear settled onto a swing.
As he swung to the sky,
a small bluebird flew by,
and his foot tapped the bird's tiny wing.

Now, the bird was a pet of the king,
and her wing really started to sting.
So she took a short string
and she learned a new thing:
She could sing with her wing in a sling.

Try Not to Blink

Let's have a contest.
You'll like it, I think.
We'll stare at each other
and try not to blink.
We'll keep both eyes open.
We won't even wink!
It's over. My eyelids
are starting to sink.

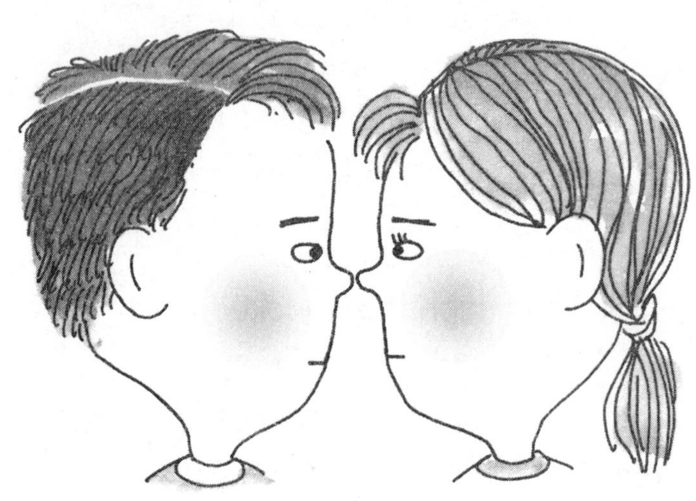

On Our Block

On our block
there is a flock
of very noisy hens.
We use a strong and sturdy lock
to keep them in their pens.
Every morn
at five o'clock
before we see the sun,
we hear them clucking loudly and
we know our day's begun.

The Mop

One morning I woke early
and found the family mop
dancing in the living room.
I couldn't make it stop.
It leaped across the carpet
and shook its fluffy top,
and all it seemed to want to do
was spin and shake and hop.

-ore Riddles

A job you must do
is a ______________.

You buy milk and eggs
at a ______________.

If something's not fun,
it's a ______________.

A sound while you sleep
is a ______________.

What Is a Slug?

Please tell me, what is a slug?
Is it a worm or a bug?
A slug is a snail.
It's slimy and pale,
and there's one on our living room rug.

Skunk in a Bunk

I stepped into my cabin,
and looked upon my bunk.
My eyes flew wide.
I raced outside.
"A skunk!" I cried. "A skunk!"

It ate a chunk of chocolate.
It sniffed through all my junk.
Without a sound,
it turned around,
and out the door it slunk.

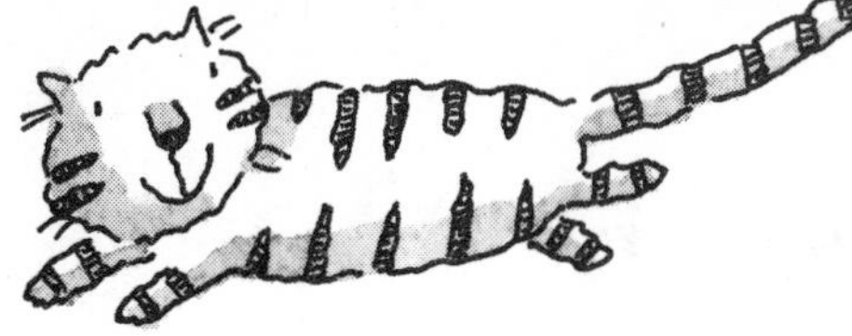

Five Vowels

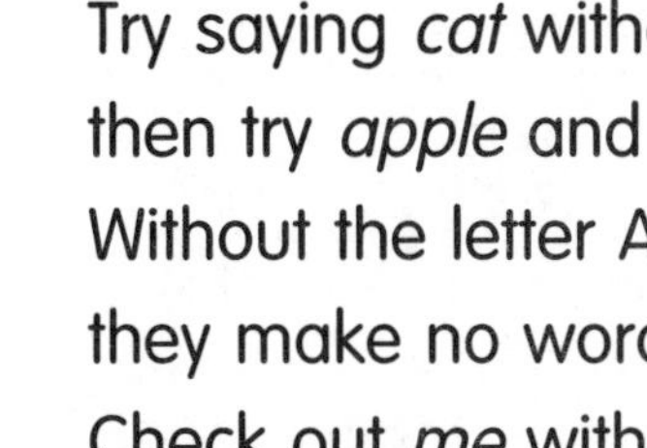
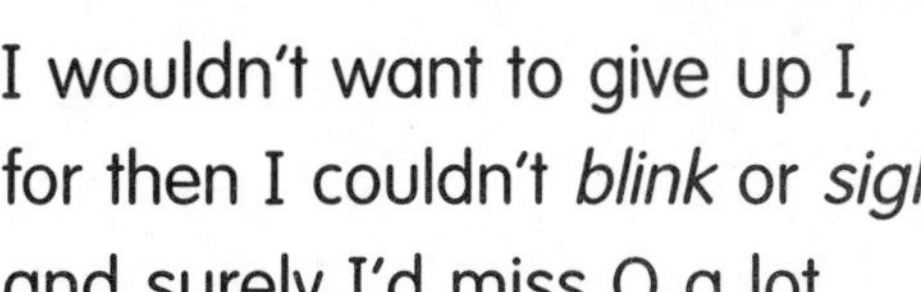
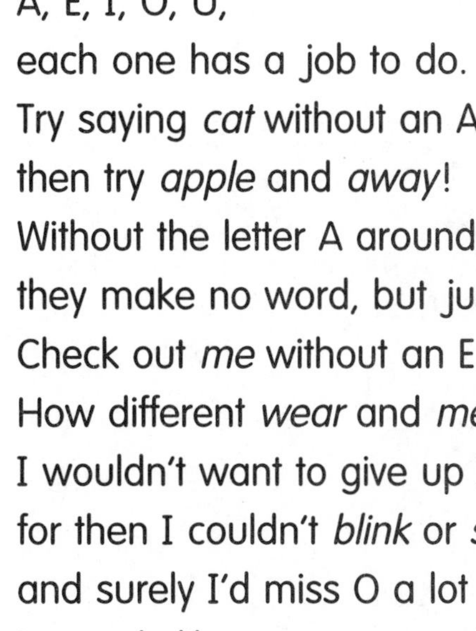

A, E, I, O, U,
each one has a job to do.
Try saying *cat* without an A,
then try *apple* and *away*!
Without the letter A around,
they make no word, but just a sound.
Check out *me* without an E.
How different *wear* and *meat* would be!
I wouldn't want to give up I,
for then I couldn't *blink* or *sigh*;
and surely I'd miss O a lot
in words like *open*, *on*, and *spot*.
I cannot say what I would do
if ever there was no more U.
There'd be no way to *run* or *touch*,
and I would not use Q too much.
I'm glad we have the vowels five;
they keep the words we use alive!

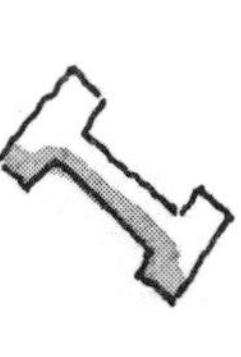
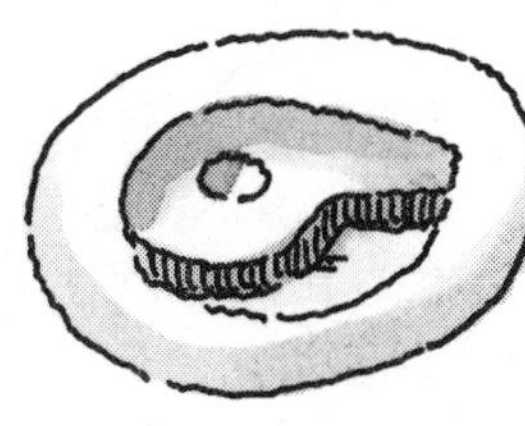

Person, Place, or Thing?

Nuts and noses, rain and roses,
Olga, oats, and Mrs. Brown,
Uncle Jim, and Arizona.
Notice these are each a noun.

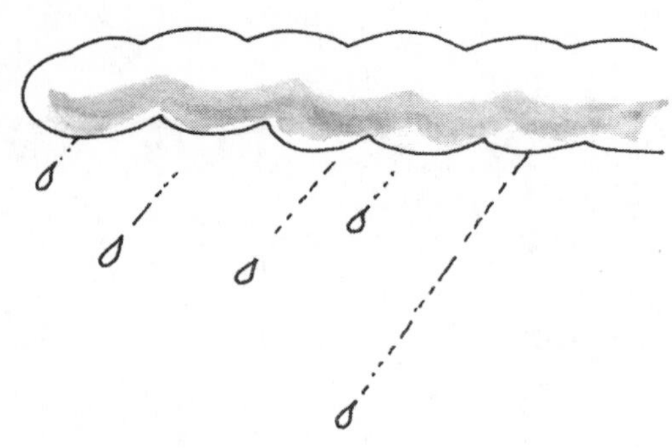

Verbs

Verbs add action and excitement.
Eat the candy. Climb a tree.
Rescue kittens. Win a relay.
Be a friend, and play with me.

Adjectives

Old and gray and happy,
sad,
light and dark
and brown,
these are each an adjective
and each describes a noun.
Silly, strong, and
wonderful,
sleepy,
dull, and round.
Adjectives describe the look,
and feel, smell, taste, and sound.

Pronoun Play

I gave it to her in the morning.
She passed it to him right away.
He gave it to them, but they'd seen it already;
they got it from you yesterday.

Seaside Homonyms

At the beach,
the sand was pale;
into a pail,
we packed it.
We quickly got to work
and built two castles there for play.
Our castles did not last an hour;
the sea, you see,
showed off its power.
A wave rolled in
and washed them both away.

Just Alike

You and I are just alike!
We nearly think the same.
You speak while I talk.
My stone is your rock.
I love. You adore.
My job is your chore.
I'm little; you're small.
I tumble. You fall.
My father's your dad.
I'm glum while you're sad.
I'm close when you're near.
You listen; I hear.
Do you know what I see?
You're a whole lot like me!

Outside Antonyms

The sun is hot.
The snow is cold.
My coat is new,
my mittens, old.
Way up the hill
and down we go.
No longer dry,
we're wet with snow.
My coat is thick,
my mittens, thin.
I'm done with out.
I'm going in.

More Than One

Change loaf to loaves
and elf to elves,
leaf to leaves
and shelf to shelves,
child to children,
man to men
but just add *s*
to pan and hen.
Deer and moose
you'll need to keep
the way they are;
the same with sheep.
Change church to churches
box to boxes,
glass to glasses,
fox to foxes,
mouse to mice,
and foot to feet,
goose to geese
and tooth to teeth.
Then turn potato
to potatoes,
as with heroes
and tomatoes,
puppy to puppies,
berry to berries,
baby to babies,
cherry to cherries.
Finally,
add *s* alone
to cup and kitten,
ship and bone.

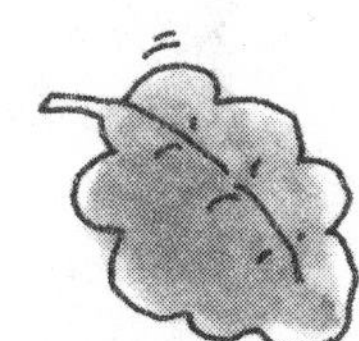

Whose Is It?

In our dad's car
on the very front seat,
we found a ten dollar bill.
None of us knew one was missing,
but everyone wanted it, still.
It isn't mine; is it yours?
Is it his?
Then whose can it be?
Nobody claimed it,
so now it is ours.
Pizza for dinner. It's free!

Outdoor Bedtime

One night at bedtime,
I stayed outside,
    there in the moonlight,
    up on a haystack,
    where it was easy to hide.
Nobody saw me
tucked out of sight,
    field for a bedroom,
    nightlight a firefly,
    telling the scarecrow good night.

Understanding Idioms

They say, "It's raining cats and dogs."
But all I see is water.
They say, "I'm in hot water," but they're not.
They tell me, "Hold your horses."
But I have no pets at all.
I'm so confused; I'm really in a spot.

A Question of Rhyme

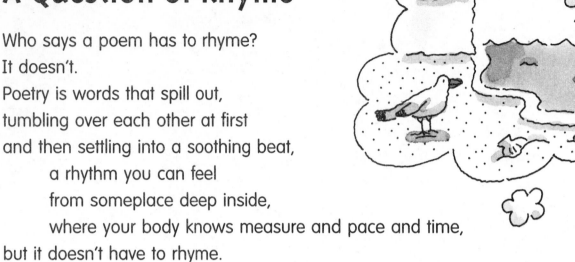

Who says a poem has to rhyme?
It doesn't.
Poetry is words that spill out,
tumbling over each other at first
and then settling into a soothing beat,
    a rhythm you can feel
    from someplace deep inside,
    where your body knows measure and pace and time,
but it doesn't have to rhyme.
Poems that don't rhyme can have
words that form pictures,
thoughts that make scenery.
Isn't that poetry?
Isn't that poetry?
That can be poetry
    too.

Paper Talk

A letter gives a way to talk
without saying a word.
Thoughts spelled out on paper
are just as clearly heard.
Beyond the date and greeting,
the page is yours to use
to tell about your work or play
or anything you choose.
When you have written all you wish,
then say a kind goodbye.
The words *sincerely, from,* or *love*
look pleasing to the eye.
The one who gets your letter
may know from whom it came
(but just in case, before you end,
be sure to sign your name).

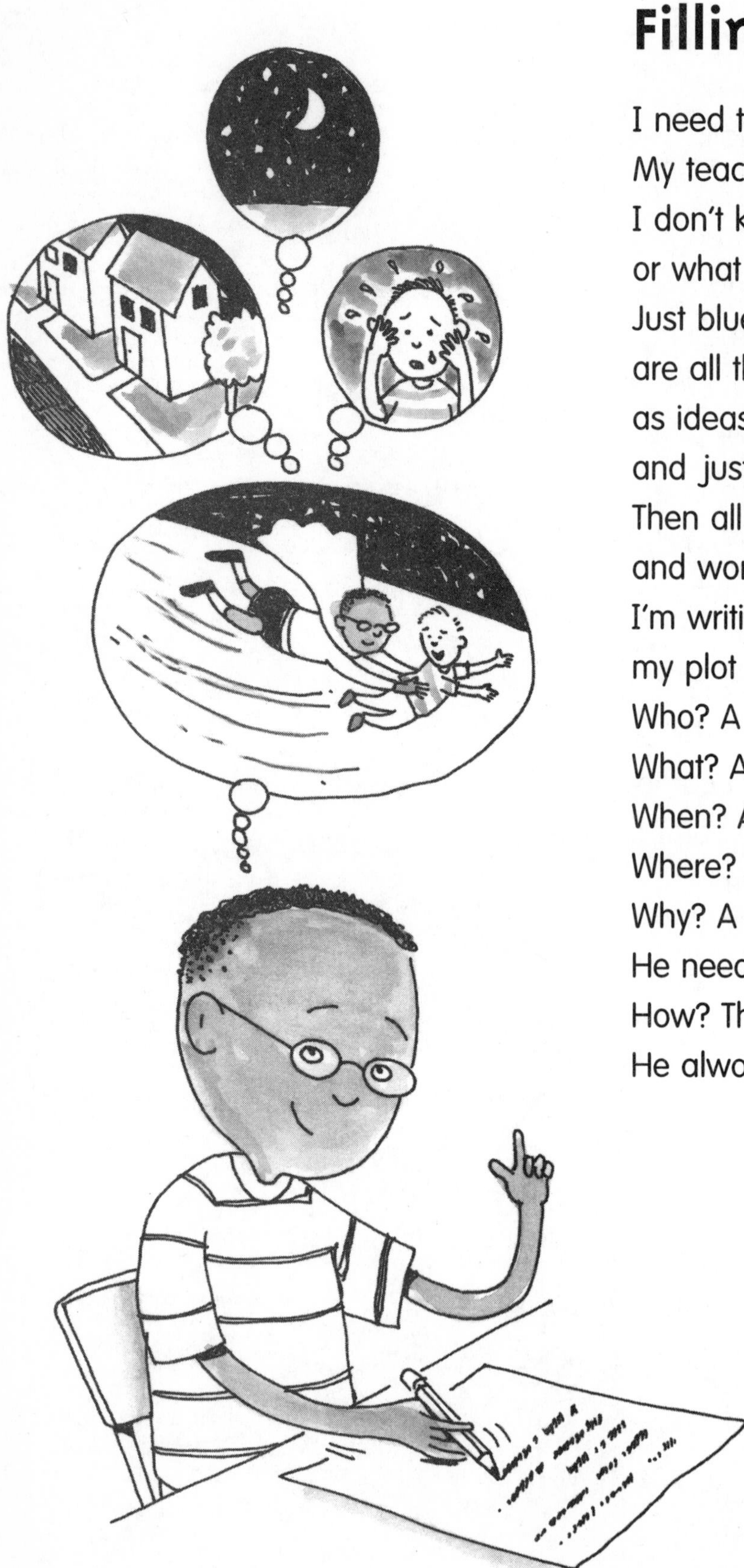

Filling in the Blanks

I need to write a story.
My teacher wants it now.
I don't know who I'll write about
or what or when or how.
Just blue lines on blank paper
are all that I can see
as ideas pop into my head
and just as quickly flee.
Then all at once, I have it
and words start to appear.
I'm writing without stopping,
my plot and ending clear.
Who? A superhero.
What? A daring feat.
When? At night, near bedtime.
Where? Just down the street.
Why? A boy is crying.
He needs help right away.
How? The hero scoops him up.
He always saves the day!

Story Trail

I opened a book
and there on its pages
were stories of foxes
and lions in cages
and forests so dark
and leafy and deep
that all who would enter
would lapse into sleep
while snakes coiled tightly
unseen on the ground
stalked uneasy mice
rushing nimbly around.
My plan was to read
just a bit to begin...
but I can't stop now,
I'm completely drawn in.

New Crayons

My crayon box is clean and new.
I look at it with pride.
Rows of crayons, sharp and smooth,
stand straight and tall inside.

Some boxes offer 48,
and 96, and more!
My teacher said I only need
the one with 24.

I count and see that there are 3
crayons that are blue.
2 are yellow. 5 are red.
3 more are purple, too.

1 white and 1 black, I see.
1 brown and 1 gray.
3 green and 4 orange ones
are neatly tucked away.

Now it's time to color, and
I want to very much,
but my 24 new crayons
look just too good to touch!

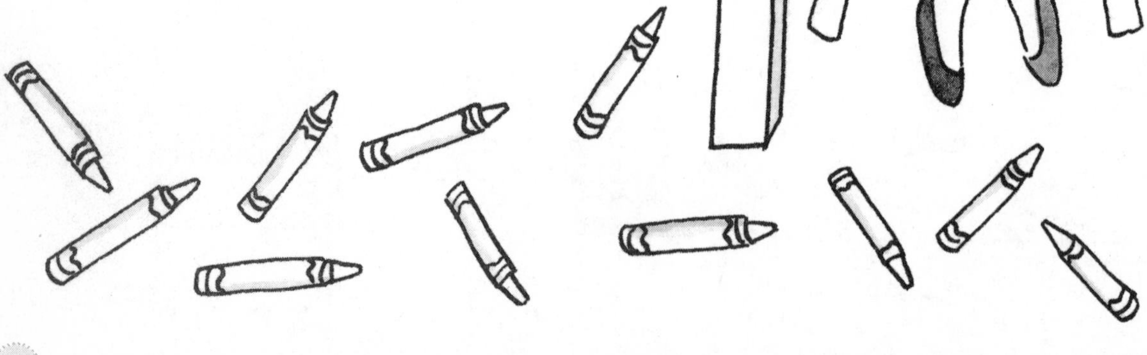

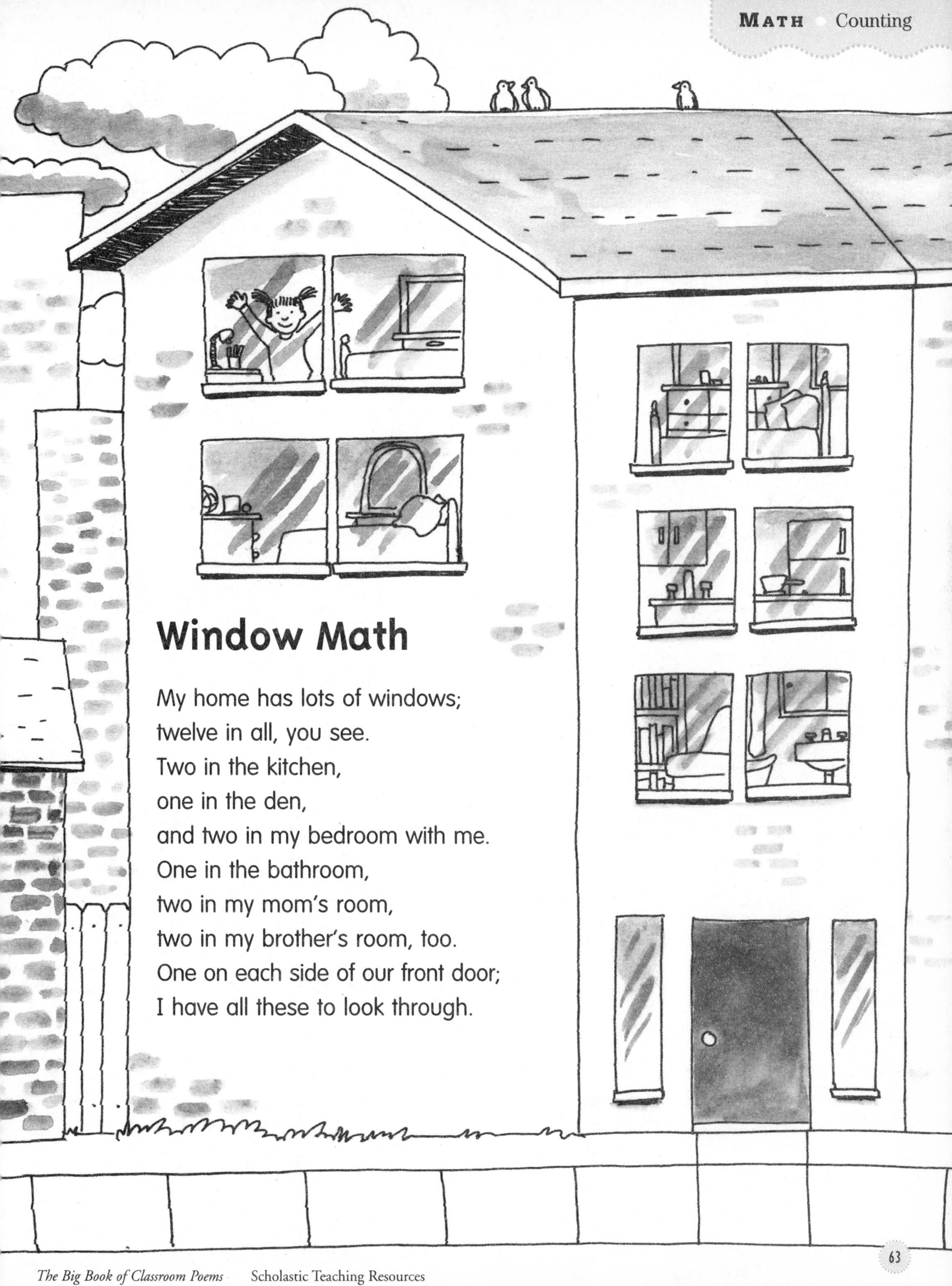

Window Math

My home has lots of windows;
twelve in all, you see.
Two in the kitchen,
one in the den,
and two in my bedroom with me.
One in the bathroom,
two in my mom's room,
two in my brother's room, too.
One on each side of our front door;
I have all these to look through.

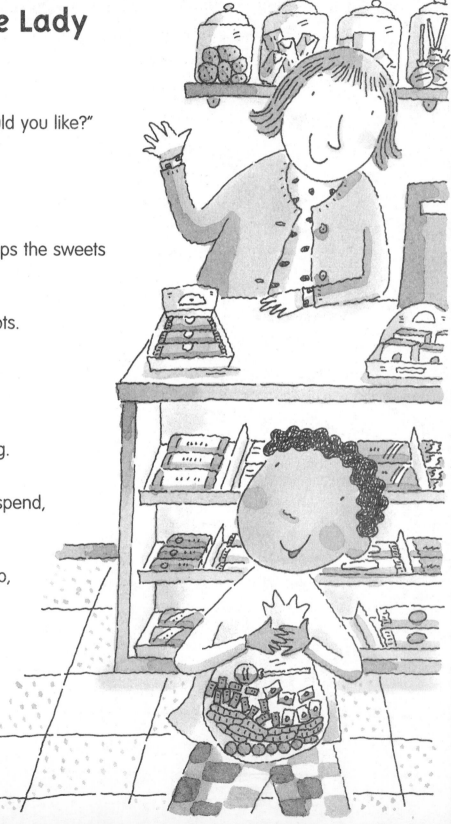

The Candy Store Lady

The lady at the candy store
seems like a friend to me.
She always asks, "What would you like?"
and then waits patiently.

Two dozen jars of candy
sit on a wooden shelf.
With plastic gloves, she scoops the sweets
that I pick out myself.

"Ten sour worms. Six Red Hots.
One dozen fruity chews."
She fills a plastic bag
with all the sweets I choose.

She's adding as we go along.
"That's sixty cents so far."
With fifteen cents still left to spend,
I spy the gumball jar!

Six gumballs and one lollipop,
and then it's time to pay.
I thank the lady for her help.
She always makes my day!

Number Families

2 + 4 is always 6
3 + 3 is, too.
1 + 5 is 6 as well.
Add it up. It's true!

6 is 7 minus 1,
10 take away 4,
9 less 3, and 8 less 2.
Can you think of more?

Schoolroom Shapes

The wall clock is a circle.
My lunchbox is a square.
An oval is the shape that forms
the top part of my chair.
My math book is a rectangle,
just like the map up high.
The reading tent's a triangle.
What kind of shape am I?

Same or Different?

I see a truck, a car, and a block.
Which one is different? Which are the same?
I see a circle, an oval, a square.
Which one is different? Tell me its name.
I see a dog, a hamster, a rock.
Maybe a slipper, a watch, and a clock?
How about a scooter, a sled, and a bike?
Which ones are different? Which are alike?

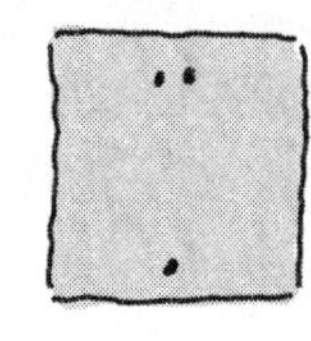

Who's Next?

John stood next to Susan
and Juan stood next to her.
Then came Lauren, Dan and Jill
and with them, Christopher.
Our class made a pattern
just lining up for gym.
If Bill was last,
who might have been
right in front of him?

Sneakers in Line

Our class took off our sneakers.
We placed them in a row.
The way we kept them on our feet
told us where they would go.
One pair that closed with Velcro straps
became the first in line.
Then came two pairs with laces.
(One of them was mine.)
Someone put his slip-ons down.
Then came a Velcro pair.
Next, two more pairs with laces
were set up neatly there.
With our sneakers all lined up
against our classroom wall,
how many of each kind had we
with 20 pairs in all?

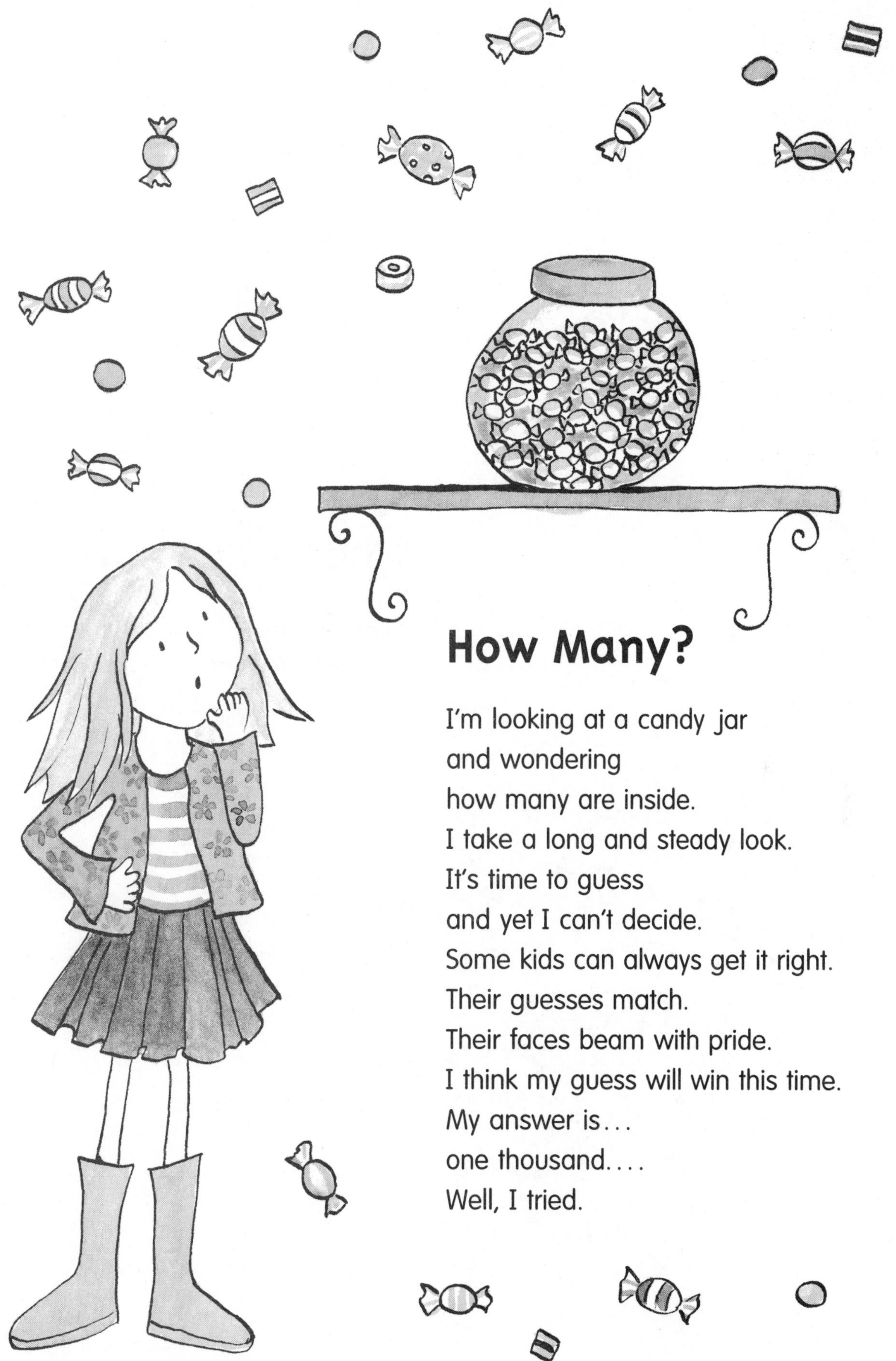

How Many?

I'm looking at a candy jar
and wondering
how many are inside.
I take a long and steady look.
It's time to guess
and yet I can't decide.
Some kids can always get it right.
Their guesses match.
Their faces beam with pride.
I think my guess will win this time.
My answer is...
one thousand....
Well, I tried.

Time Trouble

When I looked at the clock
before,
was it twenty past two,
or ten past four?

What Time Is It?

I see two clocks in the room today.
They each tell time in a different way.
One clock has a face
and two black hands
and numbers one to twelve.
We have to look at
it a while
and count out time ourselves.
The other clock is flat and black.
No hands, a screen instead.
We see at once what
time it is.
The numbers light up red.

How Tall?

Mary Ann is very tall
and I am rather short.
You'd never know I'm seven whole months older.
For when we're standing side by side,
she looks down on my head
and when I look sideways,
I see her shoulder.

Pet Pounds

The doctor tells me
that my cat
weighs 7 pounds.
Imagine that!
My dog weighs
87 now,
and must lose
15 pounds somehow.
My gerbil's tiny.
At exams,
they weigh him not in pounds
but grams.

How Long?

How long is a ruler?
12 inches, I think.
How long is the counter,
my desk, and the sink?
How far must I walk
from my desk to that door?
How long is the window?
It's six feet or more.
We all had to bring
a tape measure today.
The day seems quite short
as we measure away!

Overflow

I poured a glass of soda.
It rose up to the top.
My mother got excited.
She said I had to stop.
I stopped pouring the soda.
It rose not one bit more.
Then I put in three ice cubes
and had to mop the floor.

Thermometer

In my house,
the thermometer
gives us the final word
on whether it is
cold outside
or hot.
When I think
it is warm enough
to go without a coat,
our thermometer
often
tells my mom
it's not.

Times Tables

5 times 1 is always 5.
5 times 2 is 10.
5 times 3 is...
wait a minute.
Let me start again.
5 times 3 must be 15,
and 5 times 4 is 20.
5 times 5...
I know this one.
It's...
What's 5 plus 20?
5 times 6 is 30.
35 is 5 times 7.
5 times 8 and 9 are hard.
Ask me 10 and 11.
5 times 10 is 50;
then comes 55, and then
5 times 12 is 60.
Want to hear it all again?

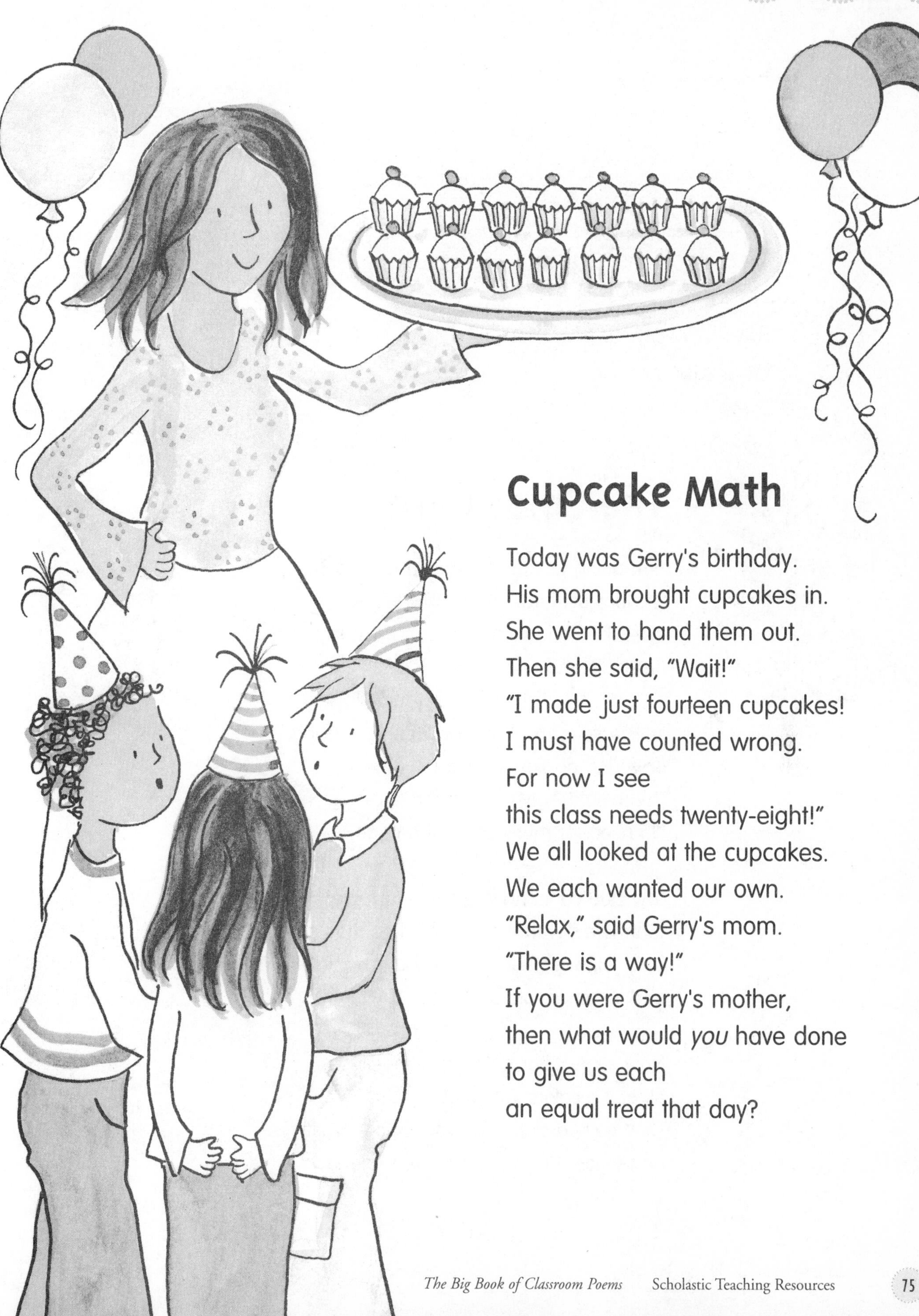

Cupcake Math

Today was Gerry's birthday.
His mom brought cupcakes in.
She went to hand them out.
Then she said, "Wait!"
"I made just fourteen cupcakes!
I must have counted wrong.
For now I see
this class needs twenty-eight!"
We all looked at the cupcakes.
We each wanted our own.
"Relax," said Gerry's mom.
"There is a way!"
If you were Gerry's mother,
then what would *you* have done
to give us each
an equal treat that day?

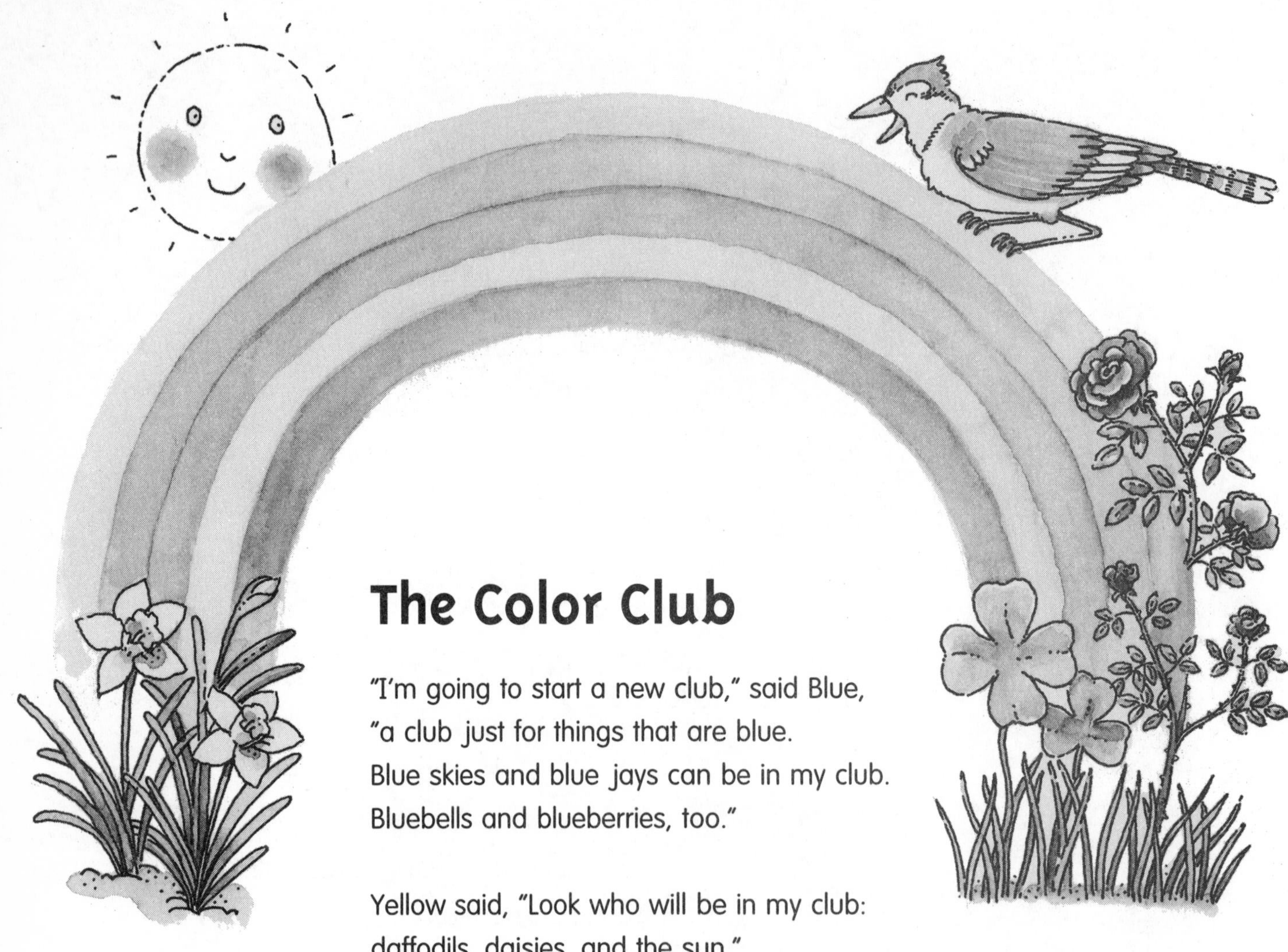

The Color Club

"I'm going to start a new club," said Blue,
"a club just for things that are blue.
Blue skies and blue jays can be in my club.
Bluebells and blueberries, too."

Yellow said, "Look who will be in my club:
daffodils, daisies, and the sun."
Green said, "My club will have clover and peas.
No need for more colors than one."

"My club could have roses and rubies," said Red.
"But here's what I think we should do:
Let's join together and form a new club
and let other colors in, too!"

Now every color belongs to the club—
all of the colors you know.
They have a club password and handshake.
And where do they meet? The rainbow!

Star

It's hard to make a star.
No matter how I try,
I just can't get the points
to come out right.
I make them one by one,
each point a different size.
They're crooked, yes,
but glitter gives them light.

Free to Draw

My pencil gives me freedom
to draw anything I want,
a comic strip,
a pirate ship,
a cat or dog,
a shoe.
No matter what I draw,
it can't be right or wrong.
It's what I see
and no one else
sees just the way
I do.

A Sticky Situation

Glue stick
liquid glue
or gel?
What's the difference?
Can you tell?
Glue stick
slides on easily
makes no puddles
hard to see.
Liquid glue
flows out so fast
pools in places
meant to last.
Gel glue
flows out smooth and clear
almost seems to
disappear.
Gel or liquid
or glue stick?
Which do you like?
Take your pick!

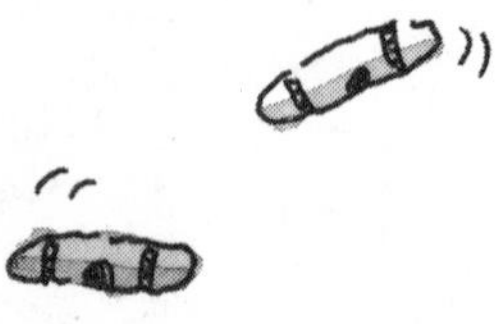

My Painting

My house might be red.
The sky might be, too.
The sun might look purple,
the grass, navy blue.
The world looks the way
I want it to be
with paper
        and paintbrush
                and color
                        and me.

Pictures of Life

a child asleep
a day in the rain
a bright, shining smile
a face drenched in pain
the depth of dark red
the coolness of blue
white wisp of a cloud
the sun's lemon hue
sailboats and sea foam
a jubilant heart
life through the eyes of a painter
        is art.

Collage

Armed with paper, sticks of glue,
and a pair of scissors, too,
magazines I cut apart
soon become a work of art.
Faces, cars, a shiny bike,
foods I eat and clothes I like,
people laughing, having fun,
chasing, splashing with someone,
ocean water, prowling shark,
fireworks that light the dark,
winter snow, and bathing suits,
cantaloupe and other fruits,
bugs disguised with camouflage...
glued in place on my collage.

Clay

Little lump of clammy clay,
feel my fingers gently play.
Push and pull and squeeze I will,
s t r e t c h i n g,
sculpting you until
you are just the shape and size
of a pair of butterflies.

Musical Muse

Music makes me feel like marching,
jumping,
hopping,
clapping,
dancing,
wiggling in my chair.
Music soothes me, makes me sleepy,
resting,
listening,
dreaming,
thinking,
peaceful everywhere.

Music ties itself to memories—
birthdays,
movies,
seasons,
travel,
holidays and such.

Music wraps itself around us,
cheerful,
moving,
calming,
pleasing,
sounds that we can touch.

The Big Book of Classroom Poems
Scholastic Teaching Resources

A World on Stage

With a script I can read
and a costume to wear,
and props
such as cups or a table and chair,
I can become someone else for a day,
as I'm living out loud
in the world
of a play.

Messy Hands

I haven't washed my hands today
or used a bit of soap.
They're getting really dirty and I know
that soon they'll be so grimy
it will be the perfect time
to leave my handprints everywhere I go.

The Magic Bar of Soap

High upon a hillside,
a prince and king and queen
did not believe in using soap.
(They were not very clean.)

Their royal hands and faces
felt sticky all the time,
and everything their fingers touched
turned gray with dirt and grime.

When they coughed into their hands,
that's where the germs would stay,
and so the king and queen and prince
were sick most every day.

Then one day, something happened.
A guest stayed overnight.
Her hands and face were squeaky clean.
Her clothes were clean and bright.

She brought with her a bar of soap.
"What is it?" asked the three.
"It's magic," said the visitor.
"Add water, and you'll see."

The king stood at the royal sink
and turned the water on.
He rubbed the soap between his hands.
"The dirt!" he cried. "It's gone!"

Everybody used the soap,
and from that very day,
they all stayed clean and healthy.
They washed their germs away.

My Loose Tooth

I had a little baby tooth
that wiggled in my mouth.
I didn't want it in there,
but I couldn't get it out.

"I'll pull it," said my mother.
"I'll yank it," offered Gran.
"Get a hanky," said my brother.
"Pull it yourself! You can!"

I wiggled it all morning.
I wiggled fast and slow.
Through snack and lunch and recess,
my tooth would not let go.

By nighttime, I was desperate.
I gave a mighty shout.
What do you think I finally did
to make my tooth come out?

Crocodile Smile

I am a great big crocodile.
My teeth are pointed, sharp, and white.
I brush them every single day,
and then I brush again at night.

To start, I turn the water on
and hold my toothbrush underneath.
I like to get it nice and wet
so it will slide across my teeth.

Once this is done, I look around
and find my very own toothpaste.
I squeeze a little on my brush.
I really like the minty taste.

Then tooth by tooth, I start to brush.
I slant my toothbrush just a bit.
I sweep the food and germs away.
My hand gets tired, but I don't quit.

I brush most gently near my gums.
I brush each tooth in front and back.
I brush in every spot I think
might be a hiding place for plaque.

When I am done, my mouth is full.
I spit the foam into the sink.
I turn the water on again
to rinse my brush and get a drink.

When I do all of this, I know
I've taken good care of my smile.
My teeth feel clean. My job is done.
I am a happy crocodile.

Bike Safety Rule Riddles

Just like a turtle,
It has a hard shell.
A ______________ could keep
your head safe if you fell.

Sidewalks are usually
safe spots to ride.
Stay back from the ______________
when you play outside.

The world looks quite dark
when you ride at night.
Be sure your bike has
a reflector or ______________.

Bikes carry people
and are lots of fun.
How many should ride on your bike?
Only ______________.

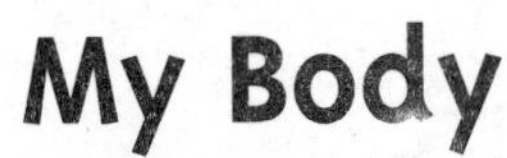

My Body

My body has a lot of parts,
and some I cannot see.
They're underneath my skin
and working really hard for me.
My heart pumps all my blood around.
My lungs fill up with air.
My liver cleans my blood
and keeps the bad things out of there.
My kidneys take what I don't need
and send it all away.
My brain controls my body,
what I think and do and say.
My stomach holds the food I eat
and makes it very small.
The best part is, this all goes on
without my help at all!

My Five Senses

I like the smell of evergreen,
and candle wax and coffee bean.
I like the taste of sour lemonade.

I like to hear my mother sing,
and cats meow and doorbells ring.
I like to look at pictures I have made.

I like to touch a flannel sheet
and feel the grass beneath bare feet.
It's pleasant and it's absolutely free.

My senses bring the world alive,
and every day, I use all five.
I taste and hear and smell and touch and see.

City Sky

Lying on my rooftop,
I can see the sky,
stretching high above me, vast and blue.

From my bedroom window,
sky is hard to see.
I look out and buildings block my view.

Down upon the sidewalk,
I feel very small.
I see only bits of blue up there.

Then I find the playground
and my favorite swing
takes me to the sky. It's everywhere!

My Place in the Clouds

I'd like to be a fluffy cloud,
a puffy cloud
of white,
the softest feather pillow
you might sleep upon
at night.
I'd like to be a skinny cloud,
a wispy cloud
up high,
a piece of cotton candy
stretching out across
the sky.
I know I wouldn't like to be
a stormy cloud
that's gray,
for I'd be full of raindrops
and I might just cry
all day.

Fog

fog is thick
and white
and misty,
drops of water
in the air,
melting snow
and slowing traffic;
fog, it seems
is everywhere.

Summer Storm

The sun shone down.
The sky was clear.
Then clouds blew in;
a storm drew near.
The clouds were dark.
They floated by.
They multiplied
and filled the sky.
Heavy with rain,
the clouds gave way,
and rain fell down
for half the day.

Rain Beat

Falling down upon the roof,
raindrops drum a steady beat.
Rat-a-tat! Rat-a-tat!
Rat-a-tat they go!
Splashing on the windowsill,
trickling down the glassy pane.
Rat-a-tat! Rat-a-tat!
Rat-a-tat they go!
Plopping in the puddles,
dripping down the drains.
Rat-a-tat! Rat-a-tat!
Rat-a-tat they go!

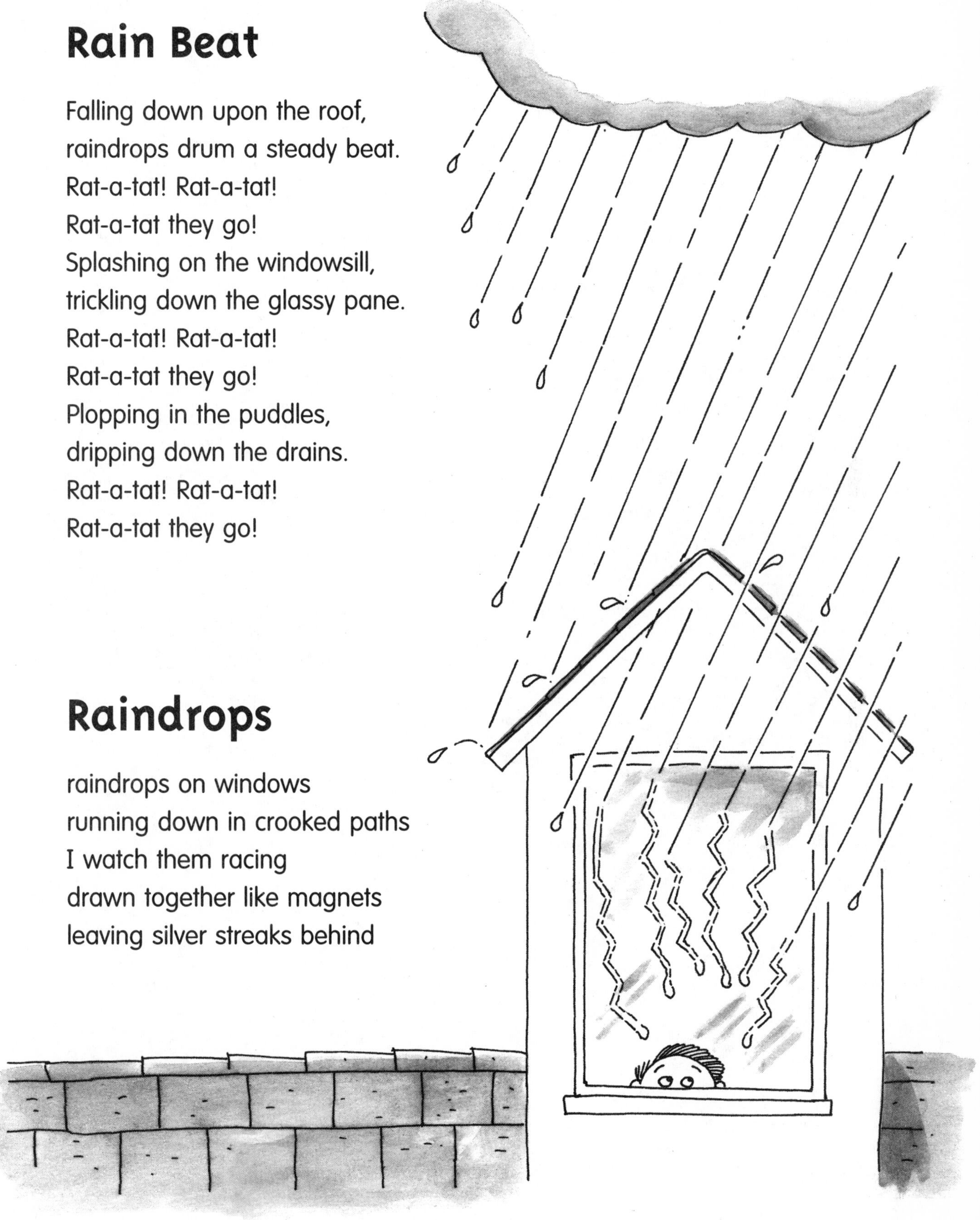

Raindrops

raindrops on windows
running down in crooked paths
I watch them racing
drawn together like magnets
leaving silver streaks behind

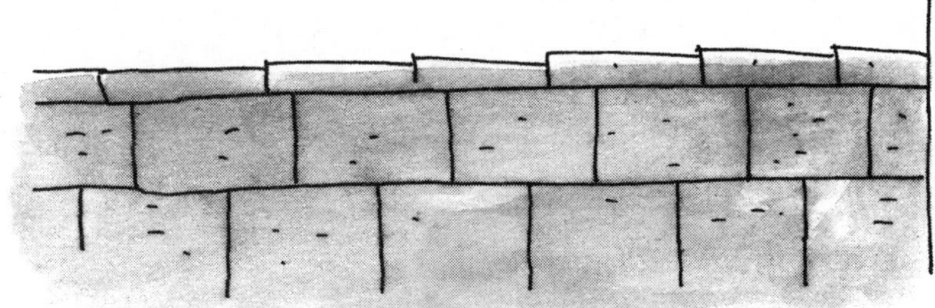

Gray Days

Soon I would like to see the sun,
not snowy days,
not all the grays,
not cloudy skies
nor drizzle.
Right now I must wait patiently,
for clouds to clear
and sun appear
and snowstorm warnings fizzle.

Hail

I like the pitter-pat of rain
drumming on my windowpane,
but I don't think it's very nice
when rain comes down as balls of ice.

Water and Ice

ice that melts into water is ice that melts into water that freezes into

Electricity

We plug in
the toaster,
the blender,
the mixer,
the washer that scrubs shirts and socks.

We plug in

computers
and TV's
and vacuums
and radios, ovens, and clocks.

We plug in
hair dryers,
clothes irons,
and fryers,
and lamps that light up what we see.

Sometimes when
I'm tired

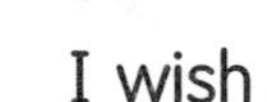

I wish *I* plugged in.

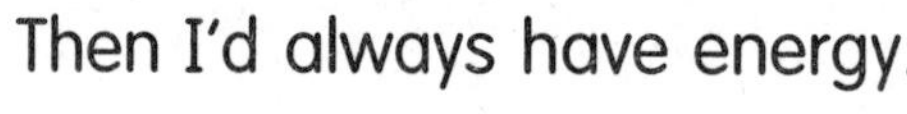

Then I'd always have energy.

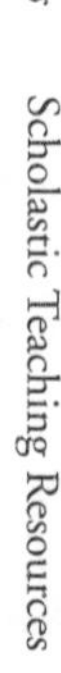

Save a Little Water

Save a little water
while you're standing at the sink.
    Use a bit.
    Be done with it.
    Never leave it running.
Water flow seems endless
as it's pouring down the drain.
    Can't replace
    what we waste.
Save a little water.

One Won't Make a Difference

One won't make a difference
if you throw it on the ground.
A piece of gum,
a plastic bag,
they're much too small to see.
ARE THEY?
One
    plus one
        a mess begun,
the one you threw
        plus others, too.
The earth, a mess
through carelessness
    that started out
        with one.

Recycle

empty glass bottles
held inside a plastic bin
tumble, shatter, crash
dumped into a street machine
a hungry giant on wheels

Second Chance

plastic, glass, and cans
newspapers, wrinkled from use
changed to something new

The Sun

warm and yellow sun,
brightly streaming from the sky
sending warmth and light

The Moon

glowing silver moon
huge and round and full of light
some nights, a sliver

Moon Glow

Moon glows, beaming light
sliver in the sky at night
clear sky, stars in sight
constellations...
small... yet bright.

Stars Sparkle

Stars... they sparkle overhead.
Night is clear,
I'm tucked in bed,
gazing out my window
at a glittering display.
Diamonds scattered way up high,
brightly shine in
blackest sky...
tiny lights will twinkle
until night turns into day.

Planet Panic

There's panic in the planets
up high in outer space.
None of them feels satisfied this year.
Pluto feels too far away
and wants to change its place.
Neptune wants its clouds to disappear.

Mercury and Venus say
they're too close to the sun,
always blazing hot without a break.
Mars complains that Earth has
altogether too much fun.
How much noise can one small planet make?

Saturn wants to spin as fast
as Jupiter can go.
Jupiter wants dark rings, it appears.
Uranus says circling
'round the sun is dull and slow.
(One year there takes eighty-four Earth years.)

There's panic in the planets,
but things might never change,
even though they fuss and fume and whine.
They don't have the power
to speed up or rearrange,
for the sun keeps all of them in line.

Animal Babies

A mallard has a duckling.
A camel has a calf,
as do a cow and buffalo
and bison and giraffe.
A rabbit has a bunny,
a wolf and seal, a pup.
Cats and beavers use their mouths
to pick their kittens up.
An eagle feeds an eaglet.
A badger tends a kit.
A kangaroo has quite a pouch;
a joey lives in it.
A horse is what a newborn foal
becomes when it gets big.
A fawn grows to a full-sized deer,
a piglet to a pig.

Animals of the Air

Crow and dove and cockatoo,
albatross and owl, too,
parrot, pigeon, and cuckoo.
These fly in the air.

Animals of the Land

Cheetah, sloth, and chimpanzee,
bear and bull and wallaby,
cat and dog and coyote.
These live on the land.

Animals of the Sea

Clam and octopus, sea snail,
walrus, shark, and humpback whale,
dolphin, crab, and yellowtail.
These live in the sea.

Animal Homes

A nest,
a den,
a burrow,
a hive with honeycomb,
a cave,
a web,
a tunnel...
to animals, a home.

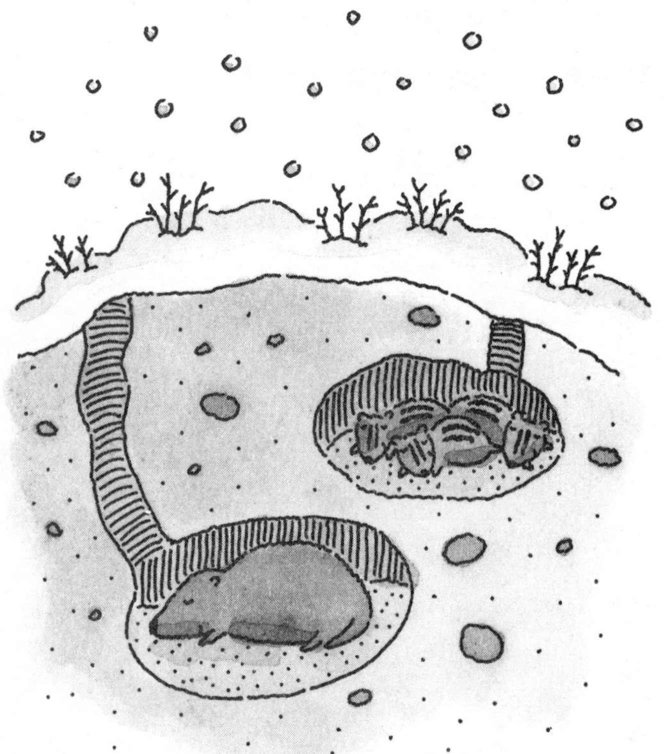

Winter Sleep

Winter is near
and the temperature's dropping.
Groundhogs and chipmunks
aren't running or hopping.
They're snuggled up,
and they'll sleep night and day,
till spring returns
and the cold goes away.

At the Zoo

If I lived at the zoo
and you came to see me,
I might be the monkey
who swings in the tree.

I might be the lion
who roars at the crowd
or just the hyena
who's laughing out loud.

I might be the elephant
swinging my trunk
or a huge polar bear
or a tiny chipmunk.

I'm all done pretending
I live at the zoo.
What would I see there
if I came to see YOU?

Where Do I Live?

I once was a camel who lived at the zoo.
One day I got out and thought, "What will I do?
I must find a place that is just right for me.
A swamp or a mountain? Now, what will it be?"

I went to the jungle to see what was there.
I felt moss at my feet and breathed hot, sticky air.
I met tree frogs and cobras, a sloth and baboon.
"This place is too wet! I'll be leaving here soon!"

My second trip was to a very cold place.
I felt ice on the ground and cold wind in my face.
I saw polar bears, puffins, and more than one fox.
"No camel could live here!" I told a musk ox.

Continued on next page.

I needed some heat, and I needed it now,
but I ended up deep in the ocean somehow.
I saw dolphins and sea gulls, blue whales, and a shark.
"This water's too deep and too salty and dark!"

It took me the whole afternoon to dry out.
Then I walked to a forest and looked all about.
I saw rabbits and chipmunks, bears big as you please.
"I can't find my way! There are too many trees!"

The next place I looked was quite hot and quite dry.
There were no trees at all. Just a shrub caught my eye.
At the foot of the shrub, a small porcupine sat;
beside it, a scorpion and a sand cat.

I knew as I walked there, on sand in the sun,
that this place I had found was indeed the right one.
"Neither icy nor crowded nor wet as can be.
This desert is home for a camel like me!"

City Creatures

Where do city creatures go
when they need to rest?
In a bush or leafy tree?
Which do they like best?

Many city cats and dogs
live in people's houses.
In the walls of someone's home,
that is where a mouse is.

Squirrels and birds build cozy nests
high up in the trees.
Bats hang out in corners dark,
anywhere they please.

Centipedes and other bugs
hide beneath the leaves.
Pigeons line up on the roof,
underneath the eaves.

Rabbits huddle under shrubs.
Ponds are home to frogs.
Often, skunks and chipmunks
find their homes in hollow logs.

What Animal Am I?

Chicken in the barnyard,
chicken in the pen,
eating feed and laying eggs,
also called a ____________________.

Curly tail and skin of pink,
I am called a ____________________.
I was once quite tiny.
Now I'm VERY BIG!

I am called a ____________________.
Cock-a-doodle-doo!
I wake up the barnyard
when the night is through.

I eat hay and apples,
also oats, of course.
I am tall, with tail and mane.
I am called a ____________________.

Feed me corn and clover,
hay and grasses now.
I will make some milk for you.
I am called a ____________________.

I am a ____________________.
from my head to my toes.
My soft coat of fleece
is used to make clothes.

Peek Into the Pond

One, two, three, four
wings have I.
Long and thin.
I'm a ________________.

I rest on lily pad
and log.
I'm green and shiny.
I'm a ________________.

I walk on water
as if it's a rug.
I have long, thin legs.
I'm a water ________________.

Under the water,
I swim as I wish.
I'm tiny and fast.
I am a ________________.

I carry a shell by the pond—
not a pail!
I'm tiny and slow.
I am a ________________.

Frog

In a fresh water home,
the frog rests on a lily pad,
waiting, watching
for food.
Its mouth opens wide.
Its tongue stretches out,
sticky
        and long
                and just right
                for catching flies.

Busy Bee

Buzz among the blossoms,
bustling, busy one.
Balance on a buttercup,
bathed in summer sun.
Itty-bitty bumble,
bold and brave, a bee;
how can one so tiny
scare big kids like me?

Bzzzz!

hear the buzzing noise
wings of a bee flap swiftly
humans on alert

Ladybug

red and delicate
black dots scattered on its back
tiny wings take flight

The Song of a House Fly

BUZZ!
I'm in your kitchen.
BUZZ!
I hit the wall.
BUZZ!
I'm in the bedroom,
halfway down the hall.
BUZZ!
There must be food here.
BUZZ!
I'll try to hide.
BUZZ!
I'm on the window
trying to get outside.

Why, Fly?

Houseflies make so little sense.
I'm not sure about
why they spend their inside time
finding their way out!

Night Visitor

What's that buzzing noise I hear
near my neck and past my ear?
Night has fallen. Sky is clear.
Mosquitoes are here.

Summer nights are warm and still.
My screen casts shadows on the sill.
Tiny hole, mosquito will
enter in with skill.

Big on noise yet small in size.
He won't bite if I am wise.
Only chance, they all advise:
take him by surprise.

Fireflies

Fireflies light up
the night.
ON! OFF! ON! OFF!
Dozens rise in
moonlit flight.
ON! OFF! ON! OFF!
Flat upon the hill
I lie.
ON! OFF! ON! OFF!
What a show up in
the sky!

Fuzzy Fellow

Fuzzy little caterpillar,
brown and black and thick,
crawl across the grass to me,
up onto a stick.
Chubby little caterpillar,
let me look at you.
How is it that one day soon,
you'll be someone new?

Monarch Migration

Every fall
in groups they rise,
alike in color, shape, and size.
They move as one to fill the skies,
a galaxy of butterflies.

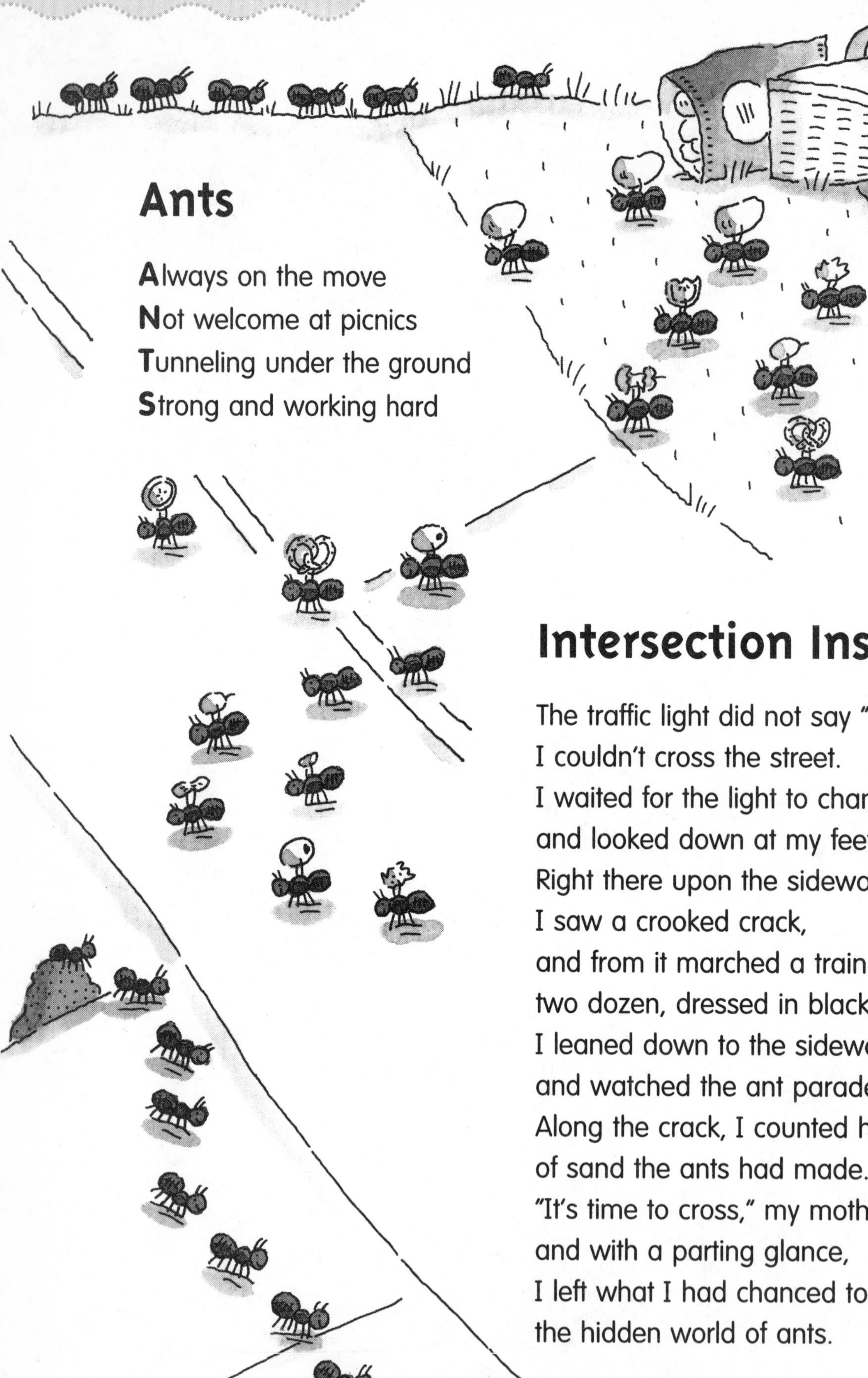

Ants

Always on the move
Not welcome at picnics
Tunneling under the ground
Strong and working hard

Intersection Insects

The traffic light did not say "WALK."
I couldn't cross the street.
I waited for the light to change
and looked down at my feet.
Right there upon the sidewalk,
I saw a crooked crack,
and from it marched a train of ants,
two dozen, dressed in black.
I leaned down to the sidewalk
and watched the ant parade.
Along the crack, I counted hills
of sand the ants had made.
"It's time to cross," my mother said,
and with a parting glance,
I left what I had chanced to see—
the hidden world of ants.

Spider

Work and weave and wind your way
'round and 'round your web today.
Silky threads together stay,
fragile... sticky... why?
In and out, in circles, too,
spinning is the job you do.
Weave until your web is through,
set to trap a fly.

Earthworm

Earthworm on the sidewalk
through a puddle trail.
I would like to pick you up.
Which end is your tail?

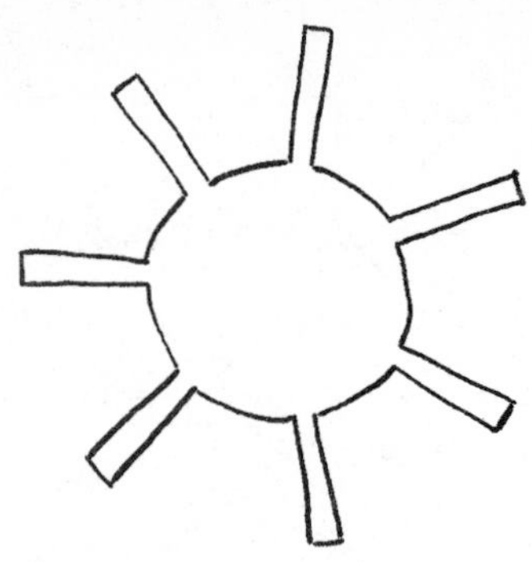

The Seed

I placed a tiny green bean seed
in soil in a cup.
I watched for it to sprout up high,
but it grew down, not up.

Then one day when I checked it out
I was surprised to see
a sprout of green poked through the soil,
as tiny as could be.

I put it in a sunny place
and watered it a bit.
A few days passed. It grew again.
Small leaves grew out of it!

Right now, the leaves are very small
but every day, I know,
if it has sun and water,
my plant will grow and grow!

Sidewalk Sprout

A little green plant has been growing.
I do not remember its name.
Nobody seems to have planted it.
It's growing quite well just the same.
It stands in a crack in the sidewalk,
one small sign of life in cement.
Although many people walk past it,
it's not even broken or bent.
I check on the plant every morning
to make sure it has what it needs.
My dad says I don't have to worry.
Plants like this keep growing.
They're weeds.

Garden Flower

A seed
a space
in fertile soil
a pat
a touch of dew
the sun's warm rays
a gardener's touch
and life begins
anew.

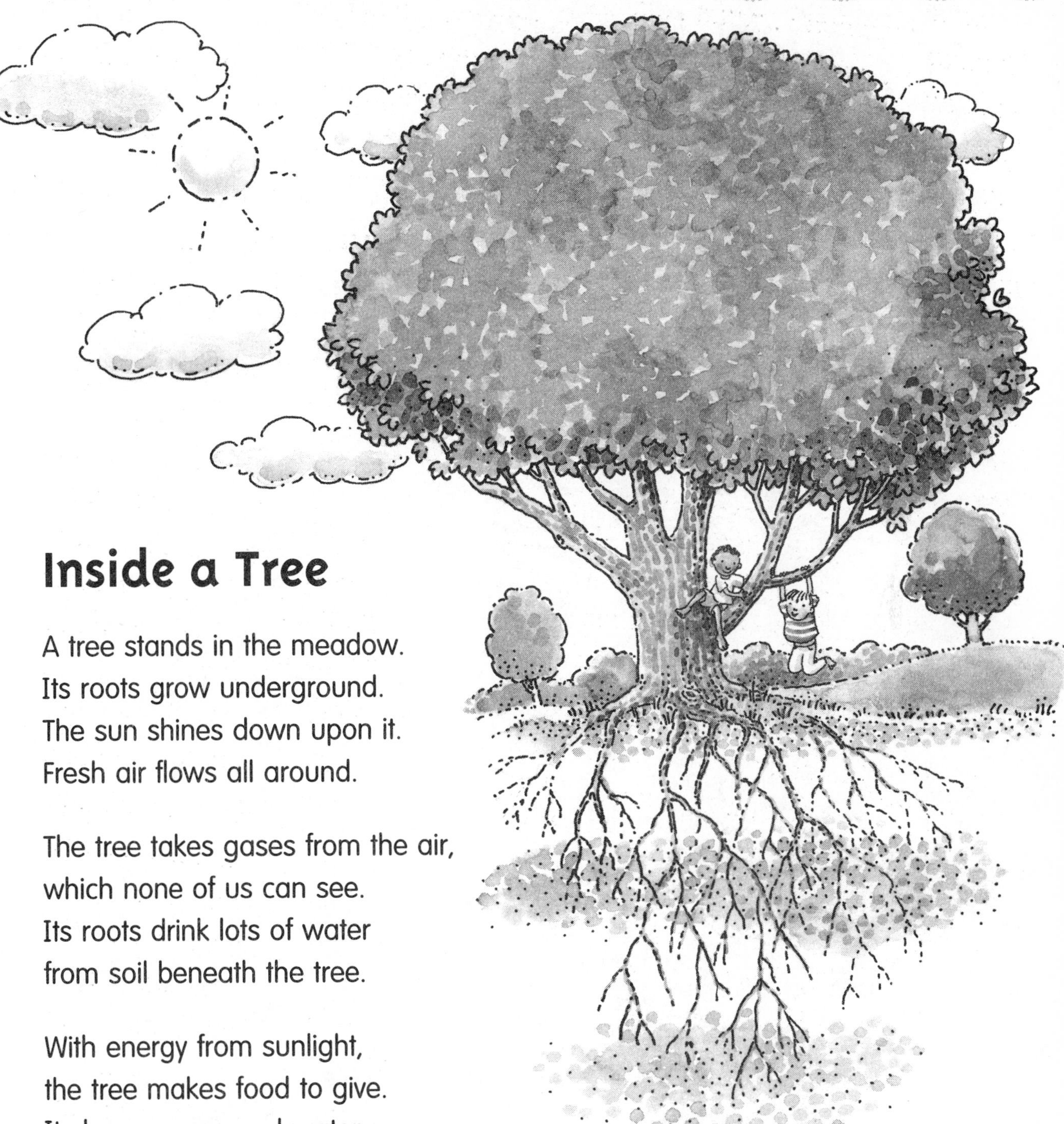

Inside a Tree

A tree stands in the meadow.
Its roots grow underground.
The sun shines down upon it.
Fresh air flows all around.

The tree takes gases from the air,
which none of us can see.
Its roots drink lots of water
from soil beneath the tree.

With energy from sunlight,
the tree makes food to give.
It changes gas and water
to food plants need to live.

The air we breathe is oxygen.
The tree makes that as well.
So much goes on inside a tree,
more than our eyes can tell.

Tree Roots

Tree roots
start out small,
creeping down
and drawing water for the tree.
Years pass,
and they grow,
stretching out
above the ground for all to see.
Sometimes
tree roots spread,
lifting lawns,
sidewalks, and streets as they grow.
Tree roots
can't be told
when to stop
nor where they are allowed to go.

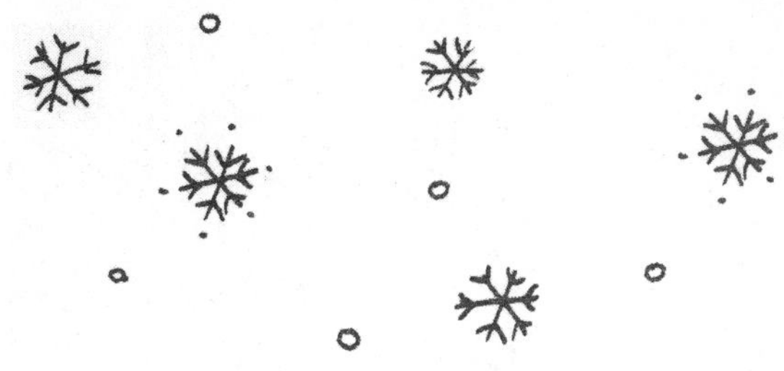

My Apple Tree

My apple tree in winter
looks cold and brown and bare.
The leaves have left its branches,
and snow is resting there.

My apple tree in springtime
grows tiny leaves of green
and beautiful pink flowers,
the nicest I have seen.

My apple tree in summer
is full of leaves, you know.
I count the small, green apples
and wait for them to grow.

My apple tree in autumn
is really best of all.
Apples now are round and red,
and they begin to fall.

Pine Tree

The pine tree seems so quiet.
The wind blows through its branches;
yet without leaves,
no rustling sound is heard.

The pine tree looks majestic,
deepest green the whole year long,
dropping pine cones
and needles on the ground.

The pine tree smells of winter,
of frosty days on the way,
of snow-covered,
powdered-sugar branches.

The Oldest Tree

I thought I had the oldest
living maple tree in town,
until the year we built a porch
and cut the big tree down.

I sat upon its burly stump
and counted, one by one,
the rings I saw upon it.
I counted sixty-one.

My tree was sixty-one years old!
That sounded old to me
until I heard that Ricky Flinn's
was one-hundred-and-three.

Autumn Wind

The autumn wind blows
and sends the leaves
dancing from the tree.
Red and green and yellow,
they twirl in front of me.
I rake them, brown and orange.
The wind blows. They are gone.
I look about, and rainbows
are scattered on my lawn.

Autumn in the Park

In the park,
we find autumn alive,
dancing with color,
inviting us to stay.
Huge maple trees
with lemon-colored leaves
tower above us,
and the sun sparkles down.
We choose a trail.
Maple trees on both sides
stretch out their branches
and touch above our heads.
Then my dad walks
and I scooter along
on a pavement path
beneath a yellow sky.

Harvest Rainbow

Orange pumpkin, apple red,
yellow corn above my head.
Pea and melon, squash and bean,
each of these is colored green.
Eggplant purple, grape is too.
What on earth is colored blue?

Pumpkin Possibilities

I bought a big, fat pumpkin,
cut out its mouth and eyes,
and made a Jack-o'-Lantern
with candle light inside.

My uncle bought a pumpkin
and much to my surprise,
he turned it into bread and muffins,
cookies, soup, and pies.

Apple Treats

Ten little apples
hanging on the tree.
Round and red and rosy,
waiting there for me.
One little apple
tumbles at my feet.
CRUNCH! I take a juicy bite.
What a tasty treat!

Hayride

Scritchy
scratchy
itchy hay
piled in a wagon,
may
I sit here beside you
while we ride around a bit?

Bumpy
jumpy
rocky ride
so much fun to be
outside
in a wooden wagon
on a sunny
autumn
day.

Scarecrow

Shirt on a stick
with a plate for its head
flaps in the wind
warning birds
to stay away
fly away
GO.

Snowflakes

Snowflakes are
crystals of ice
formed on their way
down from clouds in the sky.
Snowflakes are
pointed pictures
nature's artwork
winter's magical gift.

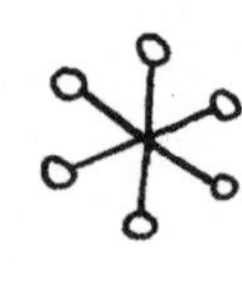

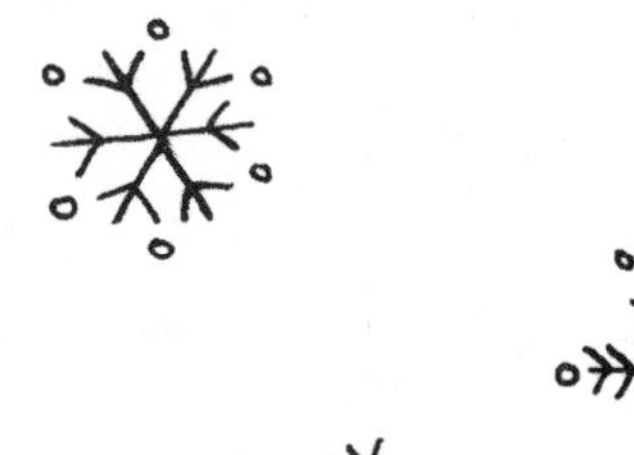

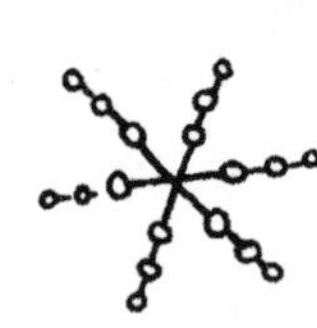

Tasting Snowflakes

Everybody says to catch
the first snowflakes of winter.
They say those snowflakes
taste the best, you see.
I've tried it every single year.
I'm missing something big, I fear,
for what I catch
just tastes like ice to me.

Winter Haiku

Winter in the Park

snowflakes tumble down
frosting benches in the park
swings hang, white and still

Smooth

snowy blanket lies
untouched by sled or footprints
earth wrapped in silence

Frost

Frost is an artist
drawing on my window,
etching swirls while I sleep.
Frost is a skater
dancing, gliding on glass,
changing my outside view.
Frost is a dreamer,
telling fairy tales
in winter white.

My Bed in Winter

My bed is my favorite place to go
when skies are dark and cold winds blow.
Under my covers, with sheets tucked in tight,
I am cozy and warm on a cold winter night.

Mittens, Hat, or Boots

I told my mom it wasn't cold,
despite what she insisted.
I didn't need my mittens, hat, or boots.
The bus stop wind has not been kind.
I wish I'd let Mom change my mind.
My ears are numb,
my fingers blue.
My toes are wet
and icy, too.
My mom was right.
It's cold out here.
I'm freezing!

Snow Sculptures

It snowed last night!
The ground is white,
and straight outside we go.
We all agree
that what we see
is perfect snowman snow!
It's wet and thick.
It rolls up quick.
Three snowmen rise today.
Our work is done.
Then comes the sun.
Our snowmen melt away.

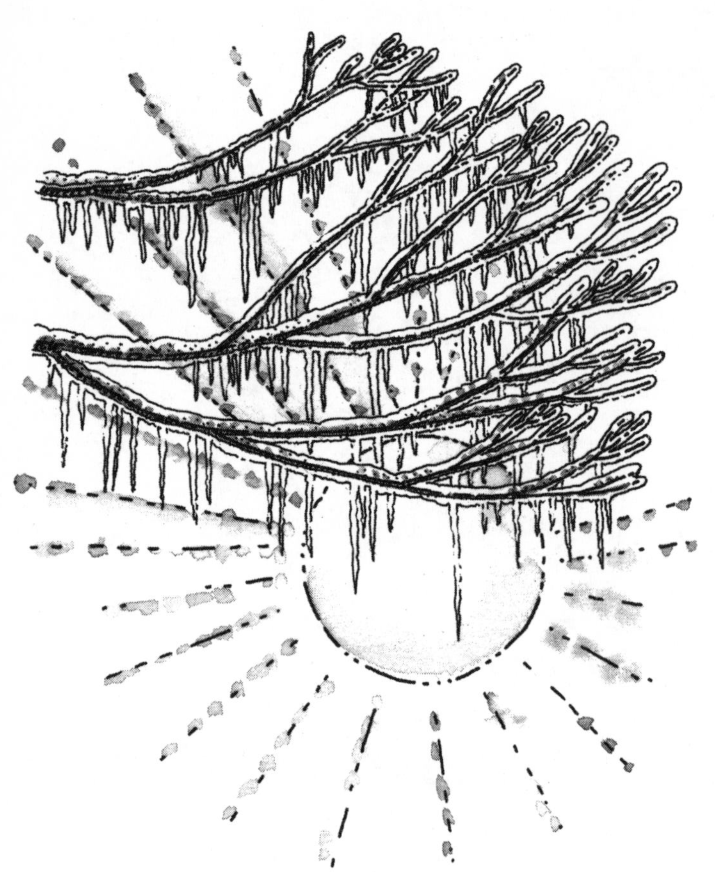

Winter Storm

rain, falling, freezing
branches wrapped in icy glaze
icicles hang down
like a crystal chandelier
all aglow for wintertime

Winter Wind

The wind blows so hard
that I cannot speak.
It's bitter and icy today.
I open my mouth
to take a deep breath.
The wind takes my inhale away.

Signs of Spring

I know that winter is gone.
Birds line up on the telephone wires.
Flowers sprout in window boxes.
Playgrounds jingle with voices.
Ducks glide on the pond,
and best of all,
baseballs thump
into my open glove.

The Coming of Spring

Last moments of winter,
first seconds of
spring
seem almost the same
and
they
blend
one into another;
the sun and warm rain
replace snow and wind
in
the
end.

Tiny Buds

Tiny buds of green
wrapped up very tight.
Come on out now, Sun!
Bring your warmth and light.
Tiny buds of green
now are leaves, I see.
Spring has worked its magic
on my apple tree.

First Flowers

Shoot of green,
sprig of life,
peeking from the earth.
Buds to follow,
flowers to bloom.
Spring has brought rebirth.

Grass

blades of brightest green
outdoor carpet, scent of spring
all at once appear

Picnic In the Park

Let's take a picnic
and head to the park,
sit on a hill, and eat lunch.
Into a basket
we'll put bread and cheese,
crackers, and chips we can munch.
Fruit juice and melon
and apples we'll choose,
cookies and pie for a treat.
When we are done
packing all of this up,
we'll be too tired to eat!

Summer Day

Summer sizzles in the sun.
Ball fields offer outdoor fun.
Sidewalks scorch uncovered feet.
Ice-cream trucks ring down the street.
Fans in windows rattle on,
cool relief when wind is gone.
Children climb and swing outside.
Metal's hot; it hurts to slide.
Trees and awnings create shade.
Stands sell frozen lemonade.
Sunshine heats a world at play
on a city summer day.

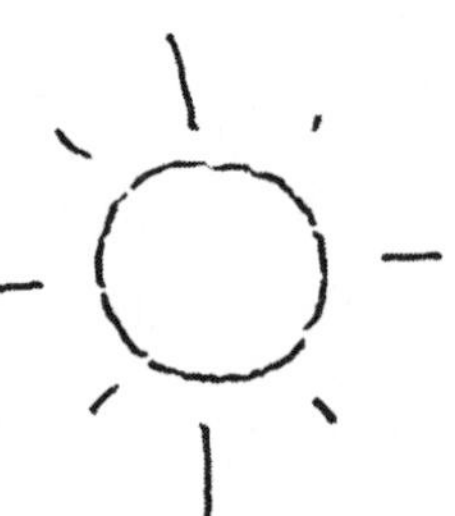

Feet Feelings

Grass tickles my bare feet.
I wander over it.
It feels cool,
soft,
and soothing.
Pavement scorches my feet.
I cannot step on it.
It feels rough,
prickly,
and totally HOT!

Summer Sports

Summer is baseball
and softball
and tag,
skateboards
and scooters to ride.
Bicycling,
swimming,
and sailing a boat,
everything fun that's outside.

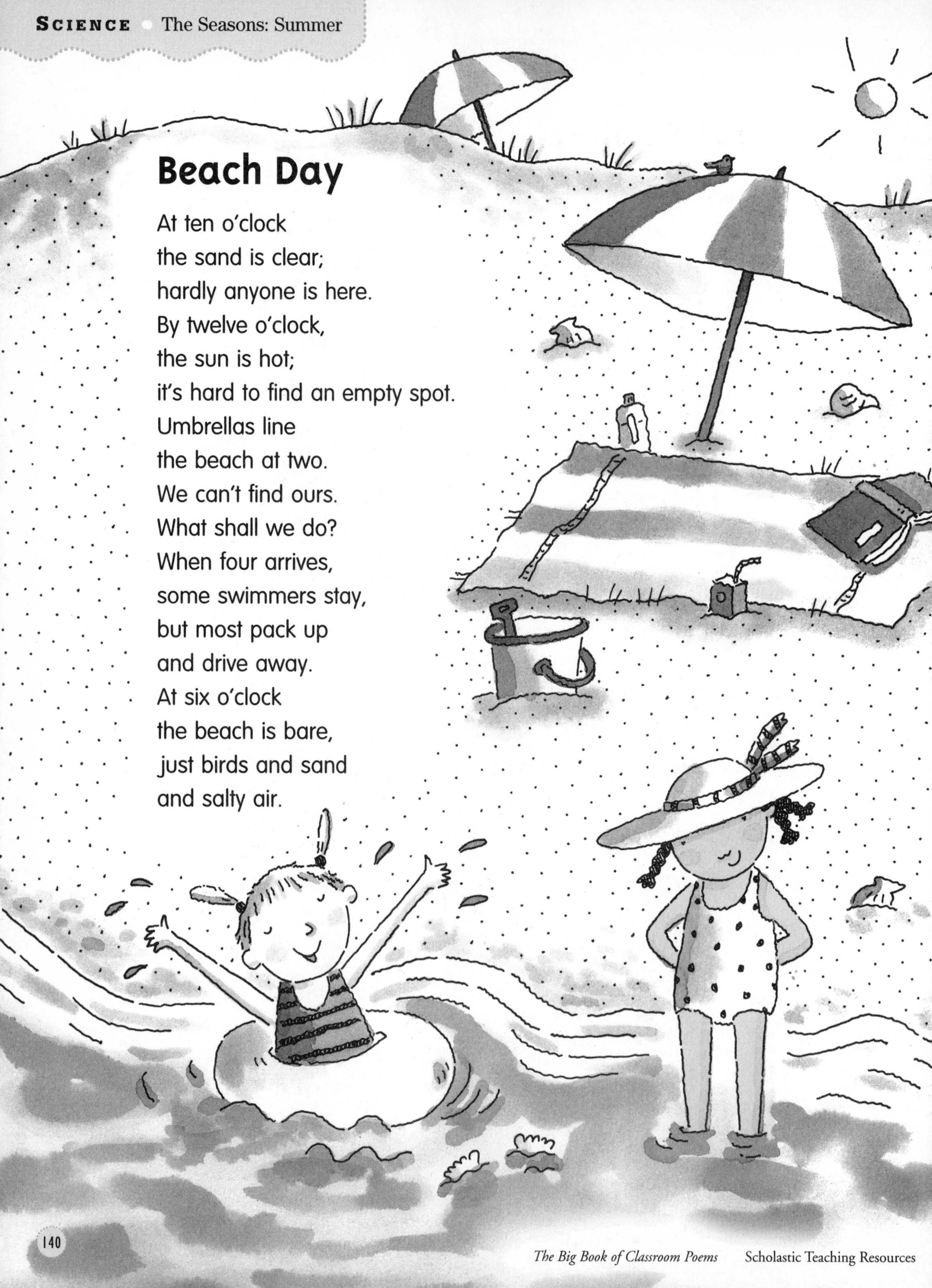

Beach Day

At ten o'clock
the sand is clear;
hardly anyone is here.
By twelve o'clock,
the sun is hot;
it's hard to find an empty spot.
Umbrellas line
the beach at two.
We can't find ours.
What shall we do?
When four arrives,
some swimmers stay,
but most pack up
and drive away.
At six o'clock
the beach is bare,
just birds and sand
and salty air.

Shells

Shells by the ocean,
round and smooth and ridged and rough,
scattered on the sand,
brown and white and pink and gray.
None are just alike.

Sand Sculptures

Build a castle with a moat.
Sculpt a car or bridge or boat,
maze or monster, birthday cake,
rollercoaster by a lake,
dragon, shark, and alligator,
dinosaur, refrigerator,
bowling alley, ice-cream stand;
each of these made out of sand.

Moonlight, Summer Night

All stands still beneath the moon,
bathed in silver light.
Only the cicadas sing
on this summer night.
Moonlight floods the evening sky.
Streetlamps can't compare
with the luster of the moon
when it's full up there.

All About Us

Our hair is brown
or blond
or black
or any shade of red.
It might be long
or short
or straight
or curly on our heads.
Our eyes are brown
or blue
or green
or hazel, black, or gray.
We're tall. We're short.
We're in between.
That's how we look today.

My Teddy

Sometimes when I am feeling sad
and things just don't seem right,
I find my favorite teddy bear
and hold my teddy tight.
My teddy's face is furry.
His eyes are bright and black,
and teddy always listens well,
although he can't talk back.

Scary Things

I'm not scared of bugs or snakes
or dogs or cats or worms.
I'm not afraid of anything
that runs or flies or squirms.
I'm not scared of thunderstorms
or wind that bends the trees,
but I don't like the darkness.
May I keep a light on, please?

A Friend for Me

Someone's in my circle
and has chosen to be there.
Someone shares a snack with me
or saves the closest chair.
Someone laughs at all my jokes
and tells me secrets, too . . .
plays with me at recess time
and likes the things I do.
Someone's fun to be around,
whatever time we spend.
Someone whom I hardly knew
has now become my friend.

Two Words

Two words come in handy
each and every day,
rolling off my tongue
as if they're all I have to say.
When I leave my coat at school,
my lunchbox on the bus,
when my homework's missing,
why, I never fret or fuss.
When the dog looks hungry
or my clothes are on the floor,
when a frosty winter wind
blows past an open door.
Two small words explain it all.
I say them without thought.
They apply to everything.
What are they?
I forgot.

Listening Ears

I'm listening. I'm listening
to your every word.
Each thought you have shared
is the one I have heard.
You have all my attention,
not merely a third.
To say I'm not listening
is rather absurd!

I heard you, but please,
would you say that again?
You had a great time
but with who, where, and when?
You must have been pleased.
Have you seen my new pen?
I missed that part.
Back up and tell me again.

What does it mean
if I look at the clock
or cover my mouth
as I yawn while you talk?
If I doodle a bit
with an old piece of chalk,
or check to be sure
there's no hole in my sock?

I do want to hear you.
Please don't walk away.
I'll stop what I'm doing
and listen today.
Though part of me screams
to go outside and play . . .
I told you. I'm listening!
Now, what did you say?

Being Kind

What does it mean to be kind?
It means reaching out from inside
to smile at someone,
to share what you have,
to cheer for someone who has tried.
Kindness can mean spending time
with someone who's feeling alone,
inviting a person
to play on your team,
or doing kind deeds on your own.
Kindness can change someone's mood
or add happiness to a day.
No matter how simple
the kind things you do,
the joy they give goes a long way.

Showing Respect

When you respect people,
you look at them
        and try to understand
                who they are inside.
You step around their things
        instead of on them.
You try to let them
        share a whole thought with you,
        even when you feel like interrupting.
You don't chew on the pencil they lent you.
        You don't lose their markers,
                and you keep the secrets they tell.
When you respect people,
        you think of the way
                you
        like to be treated,
        and that is
                exactly
        the way you treat them.

What Does It Mean to Be Responsible?

It's really very simple.
If you start it, see it through.
If you make a mess, then clean it.
Pick up what belongs to you.
If you have a job to do,
get it done before you play.
If you hurt a person's feelings,
say "I'm sorry" right away.
If you break it, try to fix it
or replace it if you must.
Keep a promise. Be a person
others know that they can trust.

Sharing

Sharing is taking what's useful to one
and making it useful by two.
It can be hard
to give up what you have,
but it shows that you care
when you do.

Cooperation

Working together,
getting along,
trying to make the whole group
really strong.
We share ideas.
We all pitch in.
Cooperation lets all of us win.

Peace

How easily a fight begins—
an unkind word...
a look...
a frown.
How sad we feel, for no one wins
when anger takes control.
We need to choose the words we say,
to talk things out...
or walk away.
It works out well for everyone
when peace becomes our goal.

Who Makes Up a Family?

A father, a mother,
one aunt or another,
a grandmother, grandfather,
cousin, or friend.
Stepdad or stepmother,
a sister or brother.
Who makes up a family?
All these, in the end.

Home

Home is more than
a bedroom and kitchen,
a place for your toothbrush,
a room with TV.
More than just shelter
from cold rainy weather,
home is a place
where you find family.
Home is a feeling,
a place of belonging.
No one can say
one is better or best.
Home is the place that your
heart wants to go to
when you need comfort,
or laughter,
or rest.

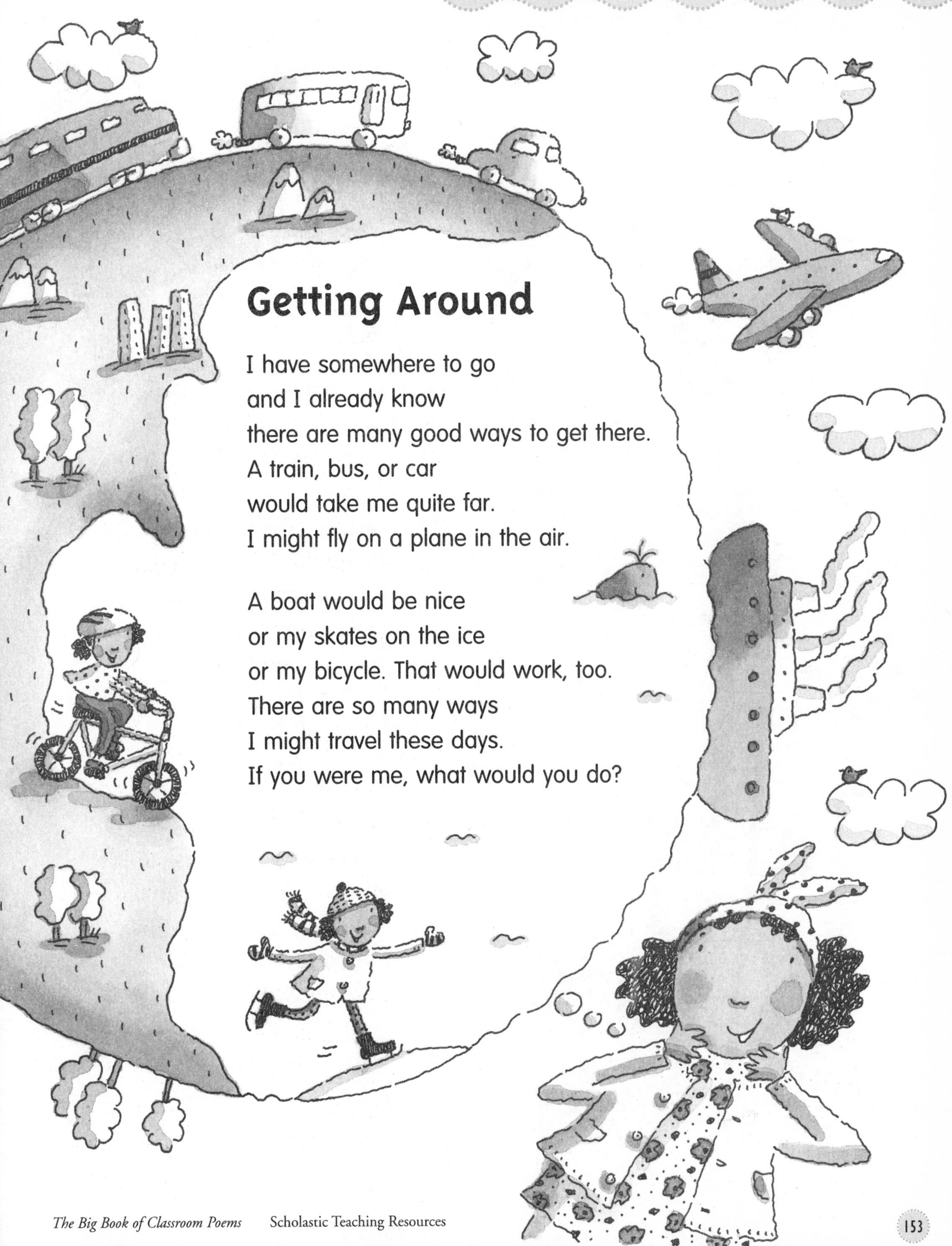

Getting Around

I have somewhere to go
and I already know
there are many good ways to get there.
A train, bus, or car
would take me quite far.
I might fly on a plane in the air.

A boat would be nice
or my skates on the ice
or my bicycle. That would work, too.
There are so many ways
I might travel these days.
If you were me, what would you do?

Subway

I stand on a platform
and hold my mom's hand.
A painted line shows me
a safe place to stand.
Down into a tunnel
of darkness I peer.
No headlights shine at me.
No train rumbles near.
The platform grows crowded
as more people come.
Will all of us fit on
the train...or just some?
Then out of the darkness
from way down the track,
I hear a train rumbling.
I take two steps back.
With a thunderous roar,
the train rushes by.
It squeals to a stop with
a hiss and a sigh.
The crowd presses forward.
The doors open wide
and squeezing together,
we all fit inside.
No seats are left empty.
I stand near a pole.
I hold the pole tightly.
The train starts to roll.
It speeds through the darkness.
I stand all the way,
enjoying my ride on
the subway today.

Where Will I Go?

I'm hungry for lunch.
I'll take a fast break
for a hamburger, fries,
and an icy milkshake.
Where will I go?

My feet must have grown.
My shoes are too tight.
I'll buy a new pair.
They'll fit just right!
Where will I go?

Books of every shape and size
fill shelves large and small.
I will find the ones I want,
and I'll read them all!
Where will I go?

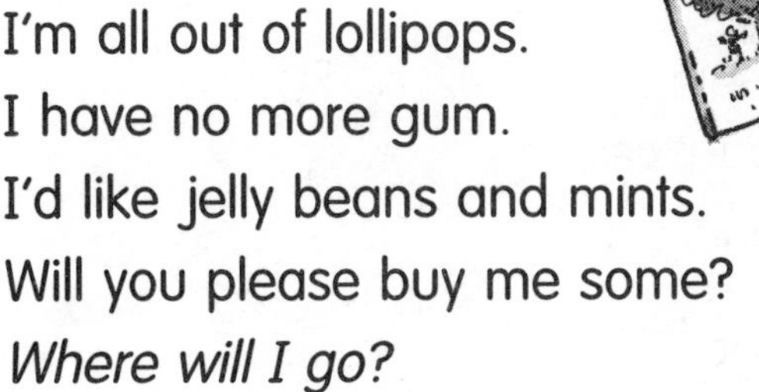

I'm all out of lollipops.
I have no more gum.
I'd like jelly beans and mints.
Will you please buy me some?
Where will I go?

I have no bread
to make my lunch.
I'll go and buy
some food to munch.
Where will I go?

My clothes are dirty.
I have no machine.
I'll take my clothes here
to get them all clean!
Where will I go?

My aunt will visit me today.
She doesn't care to drive.
Her ticket says that three o'clock
is when she will arrive.
Where will I go?

My dog needs bones
and food and toys.
When she has these,
she makes less noise.
Where will I go?

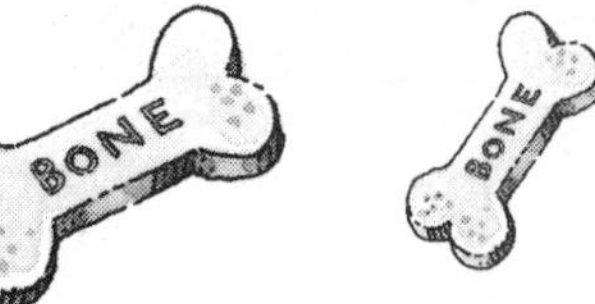

Who Am I?

Tasty cookies,
pie and cake.
There is nothing
I can't bake.
Who am I?

I like planes.
I make them fly.
I spend my time
up in the sky.
Who am I?

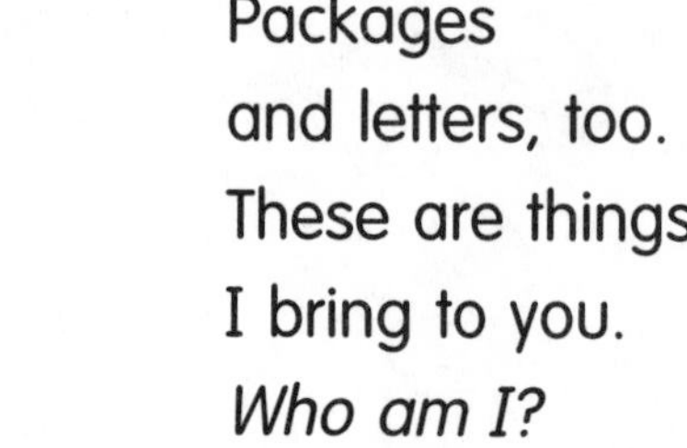

When you need
a ride somewhere
I can help.
I'll drive you there.
Who am I?

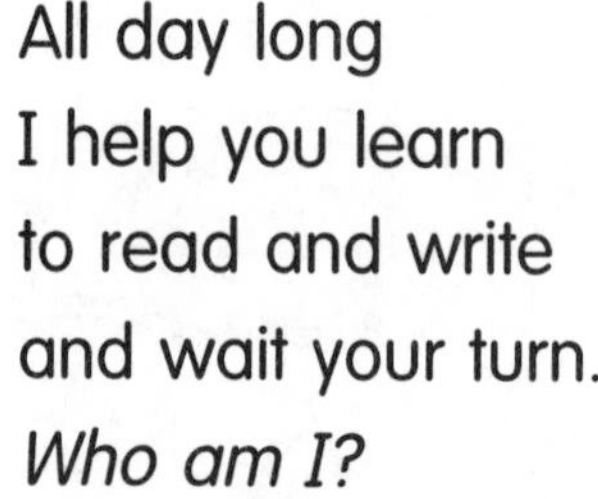

Smiles mean
a lot to me.
I help to keep
them bright, you see!
Who am I?

Packages
and letters, too.
These are things
I bring to you.
Who am I?

All day long
I help you learn
to read and write
and wait your turn.
Who am I?

Cow and horse
and chimpanzee
and dog and cat
depend on me.
Who am I?

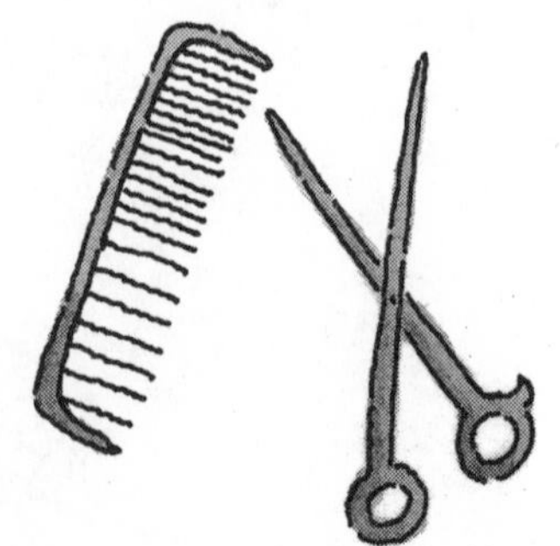

When hair is long
and you can't see,
you need a trim
and come to me.
Who am I?

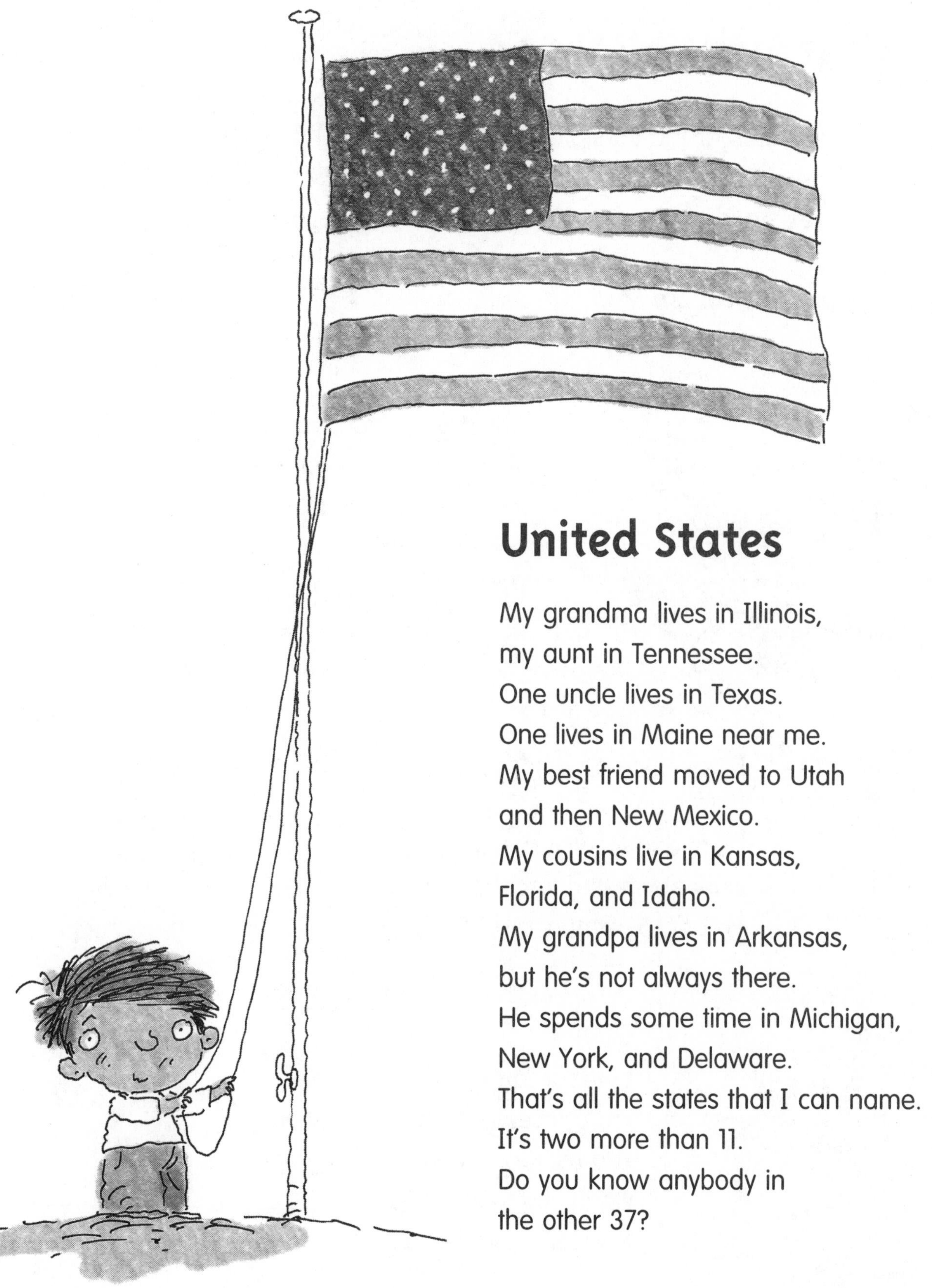

United States

My grandma lives in Illinois,
my aunt in Tennessee.
One uncle lives in Texas.
One lives in Maine near me.
My best friend moved to Utah
and then New Mexico.
My cousins live in Kansas,
Florida, and Idaho.
My grandpa lives in Arkansas,
but he's not always there.
He spends some time in Michigan,
New York, and Delaware.
That's all the states that I can name.
It's two more than 11.
Do you know anybody in
the other 37?

What Symbol Am I?

My stars stand for the 50 states
in which we live today.
My stripes stand for the first 13
to form the U.S.A.
What U.S. symbol am I?

I am strong and brave and free,
full of grace and might.
I'm a wise and regal bird,
powerful in flight.
What U.S. symbol am I?

I was once a birthday gift
from France to the U.S.
I stand in New York Harbor
with crown and torch and dress.
What U.S. symbol am I?

I wear red and white and blue.
I'm a face you sometimes see.
You think of America
when you look at me.
What U.S. symbol am I?

Where in the World Am I?

I live in a town that is part of a state
that belongs to a country
        that's one
of the countries that make up
my own continent
on an earth
        that revolves
                'round the sun.

Chinese New Year

With the first new moon
of a brand new year
comes a Chinese celebration—
time of feasting,
giving thanks,
painted dragon decoration.
In a grand parade
by lantern lighting,
dragons weave and wind and sway.
Time of honor,
time of joy.
Chinese New Year underway.

Martin Luther King, Jr.

He was a hero,
a leader,
a speaker,
a man of great courage,
and wise.
A coach
and believer,
peacemaker and preacher,
and equal were all
in his eyes.

Groundhog Day

Sleepy little groundhog,
we have long been told,
you will leave your cozy den
to come out in the cold.
If you see your shadow,
wintertime will stay.
If the sky is cloudy, though,
then spring is on the way!

Valentine's Day

It isn't the shape of your greeting
that matters on Valentine's Day.
It isn't the size of the paper
or words spelled in just the right way.
It isn't the very best drawing
or poem that will set yours apart.
What matters is just that you show me
the kindness you feel in your heart.

The 100th Day

We've counted straws and cereal
and raisins, marbles, blocks,
candy pieces, grapes, and
even fifty pairs of socks.
At last the day is finally here.
Excitement has been mounting.
We've reached 100 days of school!
Now what will we be counting?

Celebrate!

Celebrate the heroes
who stood before a crowd
and spoke of peace and freedom—
equality, out loud.
Celebrate the valiant
who found the strength within
to stay where they weren't welcome
and force change to begin.
Celebrate the leaders,
who tired but never quit
and risked their lives for freedom,
for they believed in it.
Honor all the people,
together and alone,
who stood with dignity to claim
what was their right to own.

Mr. Lincoln

Tall, thin man in a black top hat,
once in charge of a nation that
tried to break itself in two.
One, divided, would not do.
At the helm of a country wide,
stood his ground for a nation's pride.
End result, equality;
those who once were slaves, set free.
Tall, thin man in a black top hat,
leader and so much more than that:
hero, teacher, kind, sincere.
It's our gain that he was here.

History's Women

Marie discovered radium.
Amelia flew a plane.
For years, Mother Teresa
reached out to those in pain.

Elizabeth and Susan
spoke out for women's rights.
Eleanor brought wisdom
and grace to greater heights.

Jane gave opportunity
to those in greatest need.
Babe inspired women
with skill and strength and speed.

Annie taught the Navajo
to take care of their health.
Rosa proved that human rights
mean more than race or wealth.

Committed to a purpose,
they found a way to give.
Our world has been forever changed
because these women lived.

Note: The women named in this poem are: Marie Curie, Amelia Earhart, Mother Teresa, Elizabeth Cady Stanton, Susan B. Anthony, Eleanor Roosevelt, Jane Addams, Babe Didrikson Zaharias, Annie Dodge Wauneka, and Rosa Parks. (The illustrations of the women go clockwise, starting with Marie Curie on the upper left.)

April Fool's Day

This year on April Fool's Day,
I'm going to plan ahead.
I'll be the first to play a joke
when I get out of bed.
I'll write out my own list of tricks.
I'll find the best ones yet!
This year, *I'll* call out "April Fools!"
('Cause most years, I forget.)

It's Earth Day!

Grab a shovel,
pull on gloves,
come outside with me.
Pick up papers,
cans and cups
and other trash you see.
Rake the grass
or scratch the soil.
Plant a little tree.
Every effort
makes our earth
a brighter place to be.

A Time to Remember

Memorial Day
is a time to remember,
to honor and show our respect
for all men and women
who gave up their lives
for the country they fought to protect.
Although we cannot
picture all of their faces
nor recognize each person's name,
we give thanks today for
those brave U.S. soldiers.
When called by our country, they came.

Hurrah for the Fourth of July!

Hurrah for the Fourth of July,
when fireworks light up the sky!
We'll wear red, white, and blue,
share a picnic or two,
and watch the parade passing by.

Halloween Party

I sipped a cup of soda.
Black whiskers smeared my face.
My pointed ears slid off my head,
and they got lost someplace.
My gloves helped stuff the scarecrow.
That's where they both must be.
My tail ripped off in tug-of-war,
so now I'm dressed as me.

Spooky Things

I was playing in my backyard
on the grass, beside the swing.
I heard a strange and spooky sound
and saw a spooky thing.

My heart began to race a bit.
My eyes grew very wide.
This is what I saw and heard
the day I played outside.

Election Day

The candidates have spoken
and told their points of view.
They've traveled far and wide
describing what they plan to do.
They've written many letters
and shaken lots of hands.
They've answered every question.
They've told us where they stand.
The voters look no further.
It's time to have a say,
to choose the better candidate.
It is Election Day.

Veterans Day

Thank you to the people
who helped protect our nation.
On Veterans Day, we honor you
with praise and celebration.
You gave your time and effort
to keep our country strong.
We thank you, U.S. Veterans,
today and all year long.

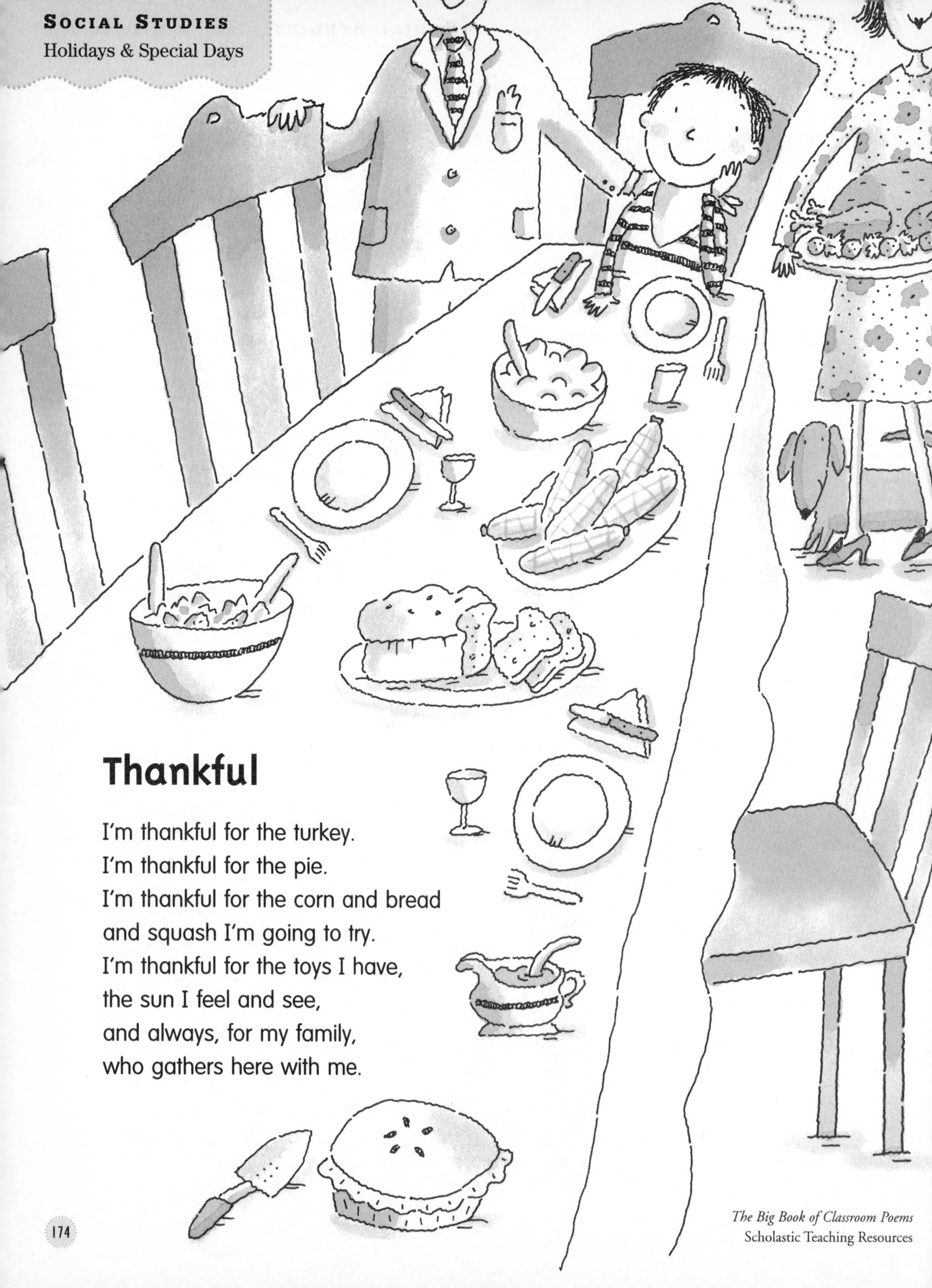

Thankful

I'm thankful for the turkey.
I'm thankful for the pie.
I'm thankful for the corn and bread
and squash I'm going to try.
I'm thankful for the toys I have,
the sun I feel and see,
and always, for my family,
who gathers here with me.

Lights of Winter Darkness

Source of warmth and inspiration,
sign of joyful celebration,
candles flicker, brightest light.
Why do they light up the night?

Los Posadas
Long parades of lighted candles,
songs, piñatas filled with treats,
honoring a family's journey
long ago through city streets.

Hanukkah
Candles in menorah glow,
Eight tall candles in a row.
Families gather and recite
blessings with each one they light.

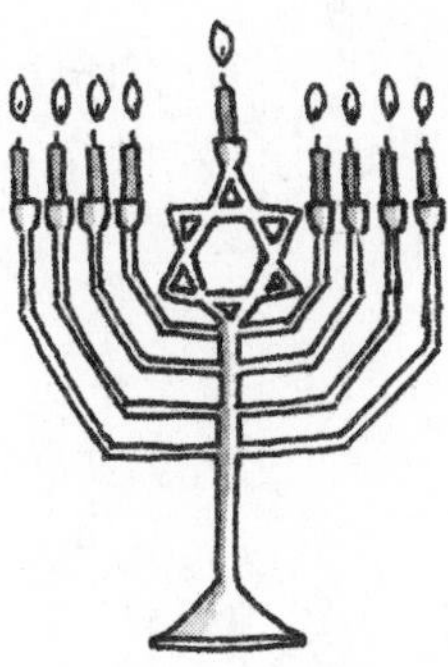

Christmas
Lighted candle in a window,
more than just a decoration,
shining light into the darkness,
light of hope and celebration.

Kwanzaa
Candles fill the tall Kinara.
Candles black and red and green.
Each one stands for something different.
Families talk of what they mean.

Birthdays by Number

One and one is always two.
Two and two are four.
Four is what I used to be;
I'm not anymore.
Four plus one is five years old.
Six is five plus one.
Next is seven. Then comes eight.
Lights out! Time for fun!

Candles

In the deepest of darkness
with friends by my side,
I wait with excitement
that's too big to hide.
Then out of the darkness
I see a bright light,
a cake filled with candles
to light up the night.
I take a deep breath and
a quick look about.
Then I make a big wish
and blow them all out.